Britain's First Muslims

Fred Halliday is Professor Emeritus in International Relations at the London School of Economics, and a Research Professor at the Barcelona Institute for International Studies. He is the author of numerous books on the Middle East, including *Islam and the Myth of Confrontation* (I.B.Tauris, 1996).

BRITAIN'S FIRST MUSLIMS

Portrait of an
Arab Community

Fred Halliday

I.B. TAURIS
LONDON · NEW YORK

6 Salem Road, London W2 4BU

175 Fifth Avenue,
New York
NY 10010
www.ibtauris.com

Distributed in the United States and Canada Exclusively by
Palgrave Macmillan
175 Fifth Avenue,
New York
NY 10010

First published in hardback in 1992 as *Arabs in Exile*

ISBN: 978 1 84885 299 0

A full CIP record for this book is available from the British Library
A full CIP record is available from the Library of Congress

Library of Congress Catalog Card Number: available

Printed and bound in India

Contents

Maps

Illustrations and documents

Plates section

Yemeni Britain: maritime and industrial communities

Preface to the Second Edition: the Creation of 'Muslim' Britain

Around the early 1990s a major shift occurred within Britain in regard to immigrants from Muslim countries and their descendants, by then totalling around one and a half million people. This shift was a consequence both of changes that had been maturing within the immigrant communities in the UK and of dramatic events in the Middle East itself. Up to this time and in contrast to the situation prevailing in other countries such as France, people living in Britain and believing in Islam were not in the main referred to as 'Muslims' but by terms of ethnic ('Pakistani') or geographic ('Asian', 'Middle Eastern') significance. However, from around 1990 it became more common to talk of a 'Muslim community' in Britain, of 'Islam in Britain' and of 'British Muslims'. After close on two decades, such terms now appear so natural and objective that it is easy to forget how recently they came into general circulation.

At the same time the widespread adoption of the term 'Muslim' in British public life posed another challenge in understanding this issue, namely how far such terms as 'Muslim' and 'Islam' – even as they do indeed define one form of identity, a set of beliefs that all Muslims share, and to a degree share much more closely than Christians[1]– may also serve to obscure or subordinate other forms of identity and association. The challenge in understanding the 'identity' of Muslims in the UK, indeed of any immigrant or indigenous community, is to gauge how far terms of religious or cultural identity – in this case 'Muslim' – are sufficient to explaining the lives and character of the groups in question. And it is in regard to this challenge that the following book, in itself a case study of a small component of the 'Muslim community' in Britain (originally entitled *Arabs in Exile, Yemeni Migrants in Urban Britain*), may serve to clarify wider public and academic debate on such questions.

As mentioned in the introduction to the original edition, this study of Yemenis in Britain (published in 1992, but based on research and travel going back to the 1970s) has a somewhat curious history. During visits in the early 1970s to what was then South Yemen, the former British-ruled territory of South Arabia, I learnt that there had existed for many years in Britain a community of migrants from that country.[2] This was something very few people in the UK were aware of, not only because of the small numbers involved but because, as I shall show later, the 'Yemenis' were never identified as such. Nor for reasons of division within their own land of origin and for reasons of convenience in the UK did they themselves at first proclaim their identity. Numbering a few thousand only, the Yemenis had nonetheless been present as a community in some of the cities of Britain since before the First World War and were therefore, apart from the Chinese who preceded them by a decade or two, the oldest non-European or 'developing world' community in the UK. The Yemenis were also the first Muslims in Britain, later to be joined by an estimated million and a half others, mainly from the Asian subcontinent.[3]

The research is an attempt to trace this history and to identify, on the basis of the contacts and sources available, the patterns of settlement, life, employment and political activities of the Yemenis in the UK in subsequent years.[4] It is also, however, a work of travel and exploration and in a very low key way an attempt to write a piece of political ethnography. This is not the only book that I have written about the history and people of Yemen,[5] but ironically, it is the only one I have written on Britain: in effect somewhat prepared, at the least made curious by my experiences in Yemen itself.

With contacts – official and unofficial – I had acquired there, I was able in some degree to gain access to these communities. The cast of characters I met – British and Yemeni – and the parts of British cities I visited were not those normally accessible to a young British researcher, 'Tiger Bay' in Cardiff, Granby Street in Liverpool 8, Small Heath and Balsall Heath in Birmingham, Attercliffe in Sheffield, the docklands of South Shields and Hull, even a *qat*-chewing den under the Docklands Light Railway in London. These were places that, without the Yemeni interest and contacts, I would never have been able to encounter. *In effect, I travelled through Britain on a Yemeni visa.*

Long invisible to British and immigrant observers alike, the Yemeni community has over recent years become much better known, and, in its own right, more visible and prominent. In the period since, in its first title, *Arabs in Exile* was first researched and published, the existence of a Yemeni community in the UK has thus come to be much more widely recognised.[6] A book/length study of the community closest to the Yemenis – the Somalis – comparing the communities in the UK and Canada has also been published:[7] while in the period covered by my research the Somalis were less numerous than the Yemenis, in the 1990s they considerably overtook them as a result of the wars ravaging their country. Figures of 200,000 and upwards for Somalis in the UK are now given, many of them refugees who came to the UK from other European countries. At the same time, as much has changed in the now reunited Yemen itself, so it has in the Yemeni community in the UK. While the major communities have become more involved in British economic and social life especially in regard to local councils, the collapse of some of the main economic supports of the community such as the steel manufacturing industry in Sheffield in the 1970s and 1980s led a considerable number of Yemeni men to return.[8] Later, tighter immigration controls at the British end and a greater reluctance on the part of Yemenis at home to permit family members to migrate, limited and in some cases reduced the numbers resident in the UK. Dr Kevin Searle, in his study of former steel workers in Sheffield, gives a figure of 4,224 for 2003;[9] informants in Birmingham in 2008 give a figure of between 10,000 and 12,000. In 2008 there were only 13 of the original Yemeni seamen still living in South Shields. At the same time, the emergence from the British school system of second- and third-generation Yemenis, fluent in English and knowledgeable about the society in which they were living, allowed a new generation of professionals and community leaders to emerge.[10]

Events in Yemen have also continued to have their impact: the optimism accompanying the unification of North and South Yemen in May 1990 giving way to the civil war of 1994 – in which the North prevailed – and to a renewed antagonism between Yemenis from North and South in Britain itself. On a visit to Birmingham in October 2007 I was particularly struck by the chasm between the two, each with their own buildings and social centres – the Northerners in one part of town, the Southerners in another.

Meanwhile, what had been intended to be a meeting place for the whole community, a building endowed by the late Yemeni millionaire Hail Said, had been appropriated by a group of Islamist militants.[11] Equally important has been the increased importance of conservative Islamic ideas and practices within the Yemeni community in the UK, this matching both what has been taking place in Yemen itself and also the prevailing trend among other, and larger, Muslim communities in Britain. However, one thing had not changed: the separation, in social, political and to some degree religious life of the Yemenis from other, often larger, communities, such as Pakistanis and Bengalis.

Increased knowledge of the Yemeni community has been compounded by a considerable increase in what has been written about the history, social structure and politics of Muslims as a whole in Britain. As in dealing with the 'Muslim world' as a single entity, and beyond the core shared principles of Islam to which all Muslims hold as a faith, the most important lesson that I would draw from the Yemeni case, as others have drawn from comparable studies is that with which I began this introduction: the diversity, plurality, individuality of the various groups that are, from the outside and by some within, classified as a homogenous 'Muslim community'. Any empirical study of particular individuals or migrant groups that are termed 'Muslim' will soon recognise differences of ethnic, linguistic, political and social character that these peoples, divided into at least 60 countries, exhibit, and the inadequacy, when not inaccuracy, of using terms like 'British Muslim' at all.[12] Here it is worth recalling the words of the noted Syrian writer Aziz Al-Azmeh on the question where he warns 'against exaggerating the role of religion in the lives of Muslims, against culturalism, against taking culture as a kind of genetic code governing the lives of Muslims, reducing culture to religion, and reducing religion to a Book'.[13]

Yet, in the light of what has later become a substantial immigrant presence in Britain, and of a literature that often unites all Muslims into one 'community', it is certainly worth drawing out what *is* generalisable, what this particular case study of the Yemenis can tell us about the history of Muslims in Britain as a whole. First, is the *historic importance* of the Yemeni case in the history of immigration into the UK and in the history of Muslims in this country. We will never know when the first Yemeni sailor set foot, or in the loosest sense 'settled' in the UK, but there was certainly a permanent presence before the First World War so the one hundred year mark must by now be past. It was the Yemenis who established the first mosques, set up the first Islamic schools and in the late 1940s printed the first Arabic and Muslim newspaper to appear in Western Europe, *Al Salaam*. The *religious evolution* of the community is also of wider significance, since while the Yemenis all remained true to the particular branch of Sunni Islam they had practised at home, of the Shafei school, the organisation and doctrinal orientation of their religious life was for a time influenced by a trend originating in North Africa, the *Shadhlilia*. The *political life* of the Yemeni community also acts as an indicator of broader trends: while for the first few decades their political activities were almost wholly dictated by the concerns of parties and later governments in their home country, they came over time to take a more active part in the campaigns of other Muslims and immigrants and also, first through local government, to engage with the institutions of British civic and political life. This was, of course, the pattern followed by the larger, Pakistani and Bengali, and to a lesser extent, Arab communities, with – it may be suggested – 1990 marking more or less the time when this transition occurred.

In terms of British public life, the presence in the UK of a large Muslim community has become a significant factor in public debate and has occasioned the publication of several studies, both on the Muslim communities themselves and on public and media perceptions of them.[14] The case study of the Yemenis – above all for the historical light it casts on issues of immigration, Islam and politics in Britain – serves to set this powerful and contemporary preoccupation in some perspective. One of the most striking features of the decades of Yemeni presence in the UK is the shifting, and always calculated, nature of the identities that they assumed or which others imposed on them. While among each other, Yemenis distinguished, and still distinguish, between those from the 'Northern' and 'Southern' parts of the country. They are also keenly aware of, and speak openly about, the more subtle distinctions of tribe, district and urban centre that mark their exact place of origin: on the train from St. Pancras to Sheffield in January 2008 with a Yemeni diplomat he was able to identify the exact district in the 'South' from which each of a group of six migrants I had photographed in 1990 had originated. In the more acute periods of internal dissension, the Yemenis have divided along fractures imported from their home country. At the same time, in dealings with British society the Yemenis have adopted, or had applied to them, a range of different categories, ones that have arisen, and been displaced, as a result of broader changes within British society and politics: from original terms such as *lascar*, *negro*, *Adeni* to *Arab*, *Mediterranean*, *Asian*, *Pakistani* and, more recently, *black*, *Muslim* and, finally, *Yemeni*. This variability between at least ten different forms of social labelling reflects not the autonomy or arbitrary character of names and discourse, some post-modern flexibility of meaning and denotation, but rather the way in which the terms applied to Yemenis were – given their low numbers – such as to assimilate them to larger categories being used at the time.

This variation in how Yemenis were termed is important to remember not only to show how many different names were applied, but also to set in historic context, and a recent one at that, the term 'Muslim', now a universally applied and apparently obvious and natural identity category in British public life. What is striking about this term is how late it became a generally used term of community, and denigration, in the English speaking world. Much has been written in recent years, in Europe, the USA and the Muslim world itself, about an ancient, 'atavistic' conflict between the 'west' and 'Islam', with Muslims cast the alien, the 'other', the ancient enemy of Europe. Current conflicts and animosities, including those in Britain, are explained in terms of this supposedly traditional stereotype. This image, largely uncontested in public debate and certainly vigorously reinforced in the rhetoric of some Islamic fundamentalists, lacks historical or analytic substance: the main 'enemy, 'other' or whatever of the British was not the distant 'Muslim', but the much more present and menacing French, German and Russian. The same is true for other European nations and for the USA.

The very acceptance of such semi-psychological categories also needs to be contested: far from there being, across centuries going back through colonialism to the Crusades, a single, hegemonic, hostile discourse on 'Muslims', the antagonisms and stereotypes of contemporary politics have in each country variant and more contemporary sources.[15] In some other European countries such as France the term 'Muslim' has been applied for many decades to refer both to the inhabitants of French North Africa, and to those migrants into France who come from there. In the British case, however, both colonial and post-colonial or immigrant terminology seemed for long to avoid the term, or use it as a pejorative or categorising word in exceptional cases such as the Indian 'Mutiny' or National Uprising of 1857.[16] One reason for this curious silence may be that throughout the long history of colonial wars that the British fought, from the eighteenth century onwards the enemies were nearly always not Muslims and at least in the cases of Palestine, Malaya and Cyprus were actively hostile to them: on the list that includes American colonists, South African Boers, Irish Fenians and nationalists, Zionist paramilitary and terrorist groups, Malayan communists, Greek Cypriots of EOKA, few were against foes explicitly cast as Muslims (the Somalis, Sudanese and Afghans being perhaps the three main exceptions). Rarely in this history of empire did the British face an insurrection from within an area under their control that was wholly or mainly composed of Muslims.

This colonial history is one, among others, of the reasons why, until as late as the 1980s, the term 'Muslim' was not a prominent term – either of self-definition or antagonistic denotation – in British social and political life. In a discourse where 'immigrants', 'blacks', 'Pakistanis' were often excoriated, where generic terms of abuse like 'dago' or 'wog' were common, 'Muslim' was largely absent, just as the term and associated claim to represent a community, was little used by people of Muslim origin: until the late 1980s those groups which did exist were in large measure the British affiliates of Pakistani or Bengali political parties, not groups claiming to represent Muslims in the UK itself. Much as such terms today present themselves as natural and eternal assertions of an identity that has always been there, all identity categories require examination of their historic origins, and of the particular time and conditions under which they emerged.

In the case of the term 'Muslim' in British public life, as suggested this can be traced to the period around 1990, in particular to two events at that time which occasioned greater public debate and awareness, as well as greater self-identification: the Rushdie affair that broke out in 1989 and the conflict over Kuwait of 1990–1991 following the Iraqi invasion of August 1990. If on the former, a number of groups that emerged from within the Pakistani community and encouraged by protests in Pakistan itself sought to oppose publication of Rushdie's novel *The Satanic Verses* on religious grounds, claiming it was 'blasphemous',[17] on the issue of Kuwait, and more particularly on the justice of Britain participating with America in a war to drive Iraq out of Kuwait, the most vocal exponents of a 'Muslim' view, and most probably the majority of Muslims in the UK, found themselves opposed to official British policy and on this issue to the majority of British public opinion. It is from this moment on, when the campaign against Rushdie's novel coincided with the dispute over Kuwait, that a 'Muslim' political identity and indeed the pervasive use of the term 'Muslim' in British public life can be dated. The first time the term 'Muslim' appeared on a British census was when religious affiliation was introduced as a category in 2001.[18] This emergence of a 'Muslim' identity in the UK has indeed come to occupy a central place in broader debates on migration, integration and multiculturalism within Britain.[19] At the same time it has provided a new identity for Yemenis to be included within, or in many cases, to adopt themselves, even as it has served – often misleadingly – to give the impression of a coherent community of believers linked to a shared political outlook among those in Britain who profess themselves as 'Muslim'. Yet as this study of the Yemeni community indicates, differences of language, custom, religious practice and politics continue to divide and at times preoccupy the supposedly homogenous Muslim community in the UK.

The emergence of a shared 'Muslim' identity and politics in the period since the first publication of this book is an important development affecting Yemenis. This change of context serves as the reason why, in re-issuing this work, I have altered the title from one with a national character – *Arabs in Exile* – to one with religious connotations – *Britain's First Muslims*. However, the purpose of this change of title is intended to convey a critical message: while it is certainly designed more cogently to set the Yemeni story in this religious context, it is also intended, by identifying the distinct and historically antecedent history of this small immigrant group, to offer one means of avoiding the trap of homogenisation whereby all 'Muslims' are assumed to be one, to share politics and social practices and to be defined, solely or uniquely, by their religious affiliation.

The story of this book, and the briefest of direct contact with the Yemeni or other such communities, shows that beyond the tenacious and universal proclamation of a set of core religious beliefs such homogenisation is a delusion. As the saying, or *hadith*, of the Prophet Muhammad so eloquently puts it: *ikhtilaf ummati rahma*, 'the diversity of my community is a blessing'.

Fred Halliday, ICREA Research Professor, Barcelona Institute of International Studies (IBEI).

Notes

1. The differences of doctrine and ceremonial practice between Sunni and Shiite Muslims are small, far less than those between, say, Catholics, Protestants and Baptists in Christianity.
2. Until May 1990 what is today the Republic of Yemen or simply 'Yemen' was divided into two separate states, the Yemen Arabic Republic, or 'North Yemen', with its capital in Sanaa, and the People's Democratic Republic of Yemen, or 'South Yemen', with its capital in Aden. Many of the Yemenis who came to the UK as sailors and, later, industrial workers, were in fact from the 'North', but had by various means acquired relevant papers in the 'South'.
3. Certainly, individuals from the colonial world including Africa, South Asia and the Middle East had visited and resided in the UK from the eighteenth century but settled and continuous communities of Chinese, then Yemenis, date from the late-nineteenth century.
4. As explained in the introduction to the first edition, the research into Yemenis was part of a broader project funded by the Arab League in London and aimed at studying and documenting different 'Arab' communities in Britain in the early 1970s. A chapter on the first Arabic-speaking immigrants, the Lebanese cotton merchants who settled in Manchester from the 1840s was published as 'The *Millet* of Manchester: Arab Merchants and the Cotton Trade' *British Journal of Middle East Studies, vol. 19, no. 2 1992*, reprinted in my *Nation and Religion in the Middle East*, London: Saqi, 2000. A final, unpublished chapter attempted to describe the Arabs in London – from Palestinians who came after the 1948–9 war to the first waves of visitors from the oil-producing Gulf states in the 1970s. The large flow of Gulf Arabs to London dates from the early 1970s: by contrast, writing of London in the late 1940s, when learning Arabic and wishing to meet Arabs, Sir James Craig was later to write that in these years he could meet only three ('Diplomatic Changes' in 'Memories of the Middle East in London', *The Middle East in London*, vol. 4, no. 9, April 2008 London Middle East Institute, SOAS). When, in Cardiff railway

station in 1975 I met the chief imam of the local mosque, he enquired
who I was working for. I told him the work was commissioned by
the Arab League. 'Who are the Arab League?', he asked, 'are they
Muslims?'.

5. *Arabia without Sultans* Harmonsworth: Penguin, 1974; *Revolution
and Foreign Policy. The Case of South Yemen, 1967–1987,* Cambridge:
Cambridge University Press, 1990.

6. On South Shields: Richard Lawless, *From Ta'izz to Tyneside.
An Arab Community in the North-East of England in the Early
Twentieth Century,* Exeter: Exeter University Press, 1995: on Cardiff:
Patricia Aithie, *The Burning Ashes of Time. From Steamer Point to
Tiger Bay on the Trail of Seafaring Arabs,* Bridgend: Seren, 2004;
on Sheffield: Kevin Searle, *From Farms to Foundries, Racism, Class
and Resistance in the Life-Stories of Yemeni Former-Steelworkers
in Sheffield,* Department of Sociological Studies, University of
Sheffield PhD Thesis, April 2007. Beyond its social and analytic
contribution Dr Searle's study is of great interest for the manner
in which it reproduces the speech patterns and terminology of the
first generation of Yemeni migrants. Sheffield was also the subject
of a BBC 4 half hour radio programme *Born in Yemen. Forged in
Sheffield,* transmitted 26 March 2004, presenter Alan Dein, producer
Mark Burman, and of a major exhibition based on the photographs
of Tim Smith, combining pictures of Yemenis in Sheffield and sites
and people in Yemen itself and organised by Weston Park Museum
in Sheffield in late-2007 and early 2008, 'Coal, Frankincense and
Myrrh: Yemen and British Yemenis'. The same photographs were
later shown in Liverpool. A parallel exhibition, 'Last of the Dictionary
Men', was organised in South Shields in April–May 2008: based on
photographs of first-generation settlers by artist Youssef Nabil, and of
video portraits by Tina Gharawi the exhibition, organised by Bridge
and Tunnel Productions, was accompanied by a documentary on the
visit to South Shields – including to a Muslim wedding ceremony
– of the American heavyweight boxer Mohammad Ali. For further
detail on Sheffield, see Debjani Chatterjee and others, *Who Cares?
Reminiscences of Yemeni Carers in Sheffield,* Sheffield Carers Centre,
2001.

7. Rima Berns McGown, *Muslims in the Disapora. The Somali
Communities of London and Toronto,* London and Toronto:
University of Toronto Press, 1999.

8. A curious and short-lived counter-trend particularly involving
migrants from the Shamir region of the North was noted in the early
1990s: this turned out to be the result of a passport selling racket,
involving a British diplomat in the Sanaa Embassy.

9. *From Farms to Foundries,* p. 1.

10. By far the most prominent second generation Yemeni was the
Sheffield-born boxer Prince Nassim Hamed. Born in 1974 he was for
a time World and European Featherweight champion, winning 36 of

his 37 professional fights and earning a reputation for flamboyant ring entrances and behaviour. In 2002 he retired.

11. The largest mosque in Birmingham, for years named after Iraqi President Saddam Hussein who provided funds for its construction, had after the invasion of Iraq in 2003 been renamed *Central Mosque.,*

12. One significant religious difference is that between Muslims of Sunni and Shiite sect. Here again conventional stereotypes may mislead: the image of Shiites that became common in the west after the Iranian revolution of 1979 and the rise of Hizbullah in Lebanon is of militant, bearded fighters, whereas the Shiites in Britain were chiefly middle class professional immigrants from East Africa, of Indian origin. The outspoken and courageous columnist of *The Independent* newspaper, Yasmin Alibhai-Brown, was born into this community, as were many other professional people. That their identity when they first came to the UK was also different, as 'Ugandan' or 'Kenyan' Asians not 'Shiites', only serves to underscore the multiplicity of identities.

13. Aziz al-Azmeh and Effie Fokas eds. *Islam in Europe. Diversity, Identity and Influence*, Cambridge: Cambridge University Press, 2007, p. 211.

14. Philip Lewis, *Islamic Britain. Religion, Politics and Identity among British Muslims*, London: I.B.Tauris, 1994; J. Jacobsen, *Islam in Transition. Religion and Identity among British Pakistani Youth*, London: Routledge, 1998; Tahir Abbas, ed. *Muslim Britain. Communities under Pressure*, London: Zed Books, 2005; Elizabeth Poole and John E. Richardson, eds. *Muslims and the News Media* London: I.B.Tauris, 2006; Homayun Ansari, *'The Infidel Within': Muslims in Britain since 1800*, London: Hurst, 2004.

15. This is, of course, part of a much wider debate on anti-Muslim prejudice, or 'Islamophobia' in particular, and on the formation and history of social and inter-ethnic attitudes in general. Suffice it to say here that my general argument is what is conventionally termed a 'modernist' one: it questions the historic, 'atavistic', 'collective unconscious' approach to these phenomena, such as those which identify a continuous century-long prejudice against Muslims in western Europe. My own analysis focuses on recent and political reconstituted attitudes. See 'Anti-Muslimism in Contemporary Politics: one ideology or many?' in *Islam and the Myth of Confrontation*, London: I.B.Tauris, 1995, reproduced as 'Anti-Muslimism: a Short History' in *Two Hours that Shook the World*, London: Saqi Books, 2001; "Confusing the Issue: 'Islamophobia' Reconsidered' in *Two Hours that Shook the World*; and *100 Myths About the Middle East* London: Saqi Books, 2005. For this reason, I am averse to the now widely accepted, but theoretically flawed category of 'Islamophobia'.

16. For one account, which graphically illustrates the British hostility to insurgent Muslims and *mojahidin,* William Dalrymple, *The Last Mughal. The Fall of a Dynasty, Delhi, 1857* London: Bloomsbury,

2006. Dalrymple brings out the degree of hostility to Muslims among the British in India at this time, and the widespread use of the term, even at that time, of the word 'mojahidin' to describe Muslim rebels, but also (p. 439) underlines that the majority of the rebels were Hindu 'sepoys', and that the Muslim rebels joined in later. British attempts to link the Mughal emperor Zafar with a broader 'Muslim' conspiracy were unconvincing. What is striking, therefore is how this overt denotation of Muslims as the 'enemy' appears to have been a singular instance not repeated in many subsequent colonial conflicts. Certainly, the British were to fight a number of wars in which the enemy were Muslims but in most cases they were denoted by ethnic or tribal names such as Afghans, Pathans, Egyptians etc. See Donald Featherstone, *Colonial Small Wars 1837–1901*, Newton Abbott: David & Charles, 1975. My (unresearched) instinct is that on a list of recognisable British colonial enemies, the word 'mojahidin' would – at least until very recently – have figured much lower than Mau-Mau, Fenian, Stern Gang, EOKA. In the 1950s a much-despised British foe like Colonel Nasser of Egypt was denigrated as an 'Arab', rather than as a Muslim.

17. Strictly speaking, there is no concept in Islam equivalent to the Christian term 'blasphemy' in the sense of insulting divine beings. The Prophet Muhammad was an ordinary human being and the term used by Islamic writers that is normally translated as 'blasphemy' – *kofr* – is a much broader term for disbelief, abandonment of Islam and so forth. The whole Rushdie affair, its origins and not least its consequences within the UK has to be seen in *political*, rather than religious or theological, terms.

18. Serena Hussain, *Muslims on the Map. A National Survey of Social Trends in Britain*, London: Tauris Academic Studies, 2008.

19. Tariq Modood, *Multicultural Politics. Racism, Ethnicity and Muslims in Britain*, Edinburgh: Edinburgh University Press, 2005; Peter Hopkins and Richard Gale, eds. *Muslims in Britain. Race, Place and Identities*, Edinburgh: Edinburgh University Press, 2008.

The Remotest Village

The following study has had a long period of development. My own interest in the Yemen began in 1970 when I paid my first visit to Aden, the capital of what was then South Yemen, or the People's Democratic Republic of Yemen, in connection with research I was doing on the history of the nationalist movements in the region. I was able to revisit South Yemen on a number of other occasions and, in 1984, to visit North Yemen. It was through this contact with the two Yemeni states and with a wide range of Yemenis both in their home countries and in Britain that I became acquainted with the Yemeni community in Britain and learnt about the history of their settlement and the changing social and economic conditions under which they lived.

From the mid 1970s onwards, I began visiting and recording the life of the Yemeni community in Britain and collecting what materials were available on it. It is this background which explains the material in the following study – a historical overview from the first settlements in the early twentieth century, an account of the communities in the 1970s, and a later survey of changes at the end of the 1980s. The approach combines historical record, social and political analysis and personal observation in what will, I hope, serve as a general if by no means exhaustive introduction to this community.

The title of this introduction, 'The Remotest Village', is intended to convey something of the relationship of the British Yemenis both to their country of origin and to that of settlement. Of all the groupings of Yemeni emigrants, those in Britain are among the furthest in living and overall conditions from their homeland: the contrast between the sun-drenched villages of the

Yemeni mountains and the dank Victorian streets of Attercliffe and Small Heath could hardly be greater. The Yemenis of Britain are certainly known in the Yemens themselves: in both parts of Yemen one often runs into people speaking with distinctive British regional accents, who have spent years in Cardiff, Birmingham or elsewhere. In 1977 in the mountains of Shu'aib in what was formerly South Yemen, from which many of those in Sheffield come, I found the hospital and school projects funded by the British migrants; in Ta'iz in 1984, in the southern part of former North Yemen, I came across the Sheikh Abdullah Ali al-Hakimi secondary school, named after the leader of the British Yemenis in the 1930s and 1940s. But the life and conditions of the Yemenis in Britain are particularly remote from those in their country of origin, much more so than those of the larger number of Yemenis who have migrated to the neighbouring oil-producing states.

The Yemenis are also a remote village as far as British society itself is concerned. The Yemenis in Britain are a close-knit if internally fissured community, a village-like grouping transposed from their original context into a difficult and often hostile environment. They form an 'urban village' in the sense in which this term has come to be used; a migrant community living within its own socially, linguistically and ethnically defined borders, and interacting in a selective way with the broader society around it. That the Yemenis are also 'remote' from British society is evident enough, since they are not only distinct and separated off in a variety of ways, some imposed and some chosen, but have, in ways to be discussed in the concluding chapter, been remarkably unseen by the broader society around them. This separateness from Britain began to change in the course of the 1980s, and it is hoped that this study will make its contribution to this process of greater recognition and understanding of one of the longest-established Third World communities in this country.

The list of those who have assisted me over the years is long. I should like to record a special debt of gratitude to those who had worked on this topic before me and whose accounts of the Yemeni community proved invaluable: R.B. Serjeant, Sydney Collins, K.S. Little, Badr ud-Din Dahya. Their work formed part of the early study of immigrants in Britain and covered the period up to the 1960s; if I have been able to add to their findings, it is by bringing the story up to the end of the 1980s, and by setting this community more explicitly and extensively in its Yemeni context. The initial research was carried out in 1975–6 with the assistance of a grant from the Arab League Office in London: I should like to pay a special thanks to the two people most closely involved in the decision to fund and encourage the project, Muhammad Wahbi of the League Office, and Lakhdar Brahimi, then ambassador of Algeria. Additional funding for both historical and contemporary aspects of the research was provided by the International Studies Research Division at the London School of Economics: it was the ISRD which enabled me to secure the co-operation of Dr Sarah Graham-Brown, who undertook invaluable further documentary and photographic research. Jane Pugh at the LSE kindly prepared the maps. Doreen and Leila Ingrams provided me with materials they had discovered in the Public Records Office.

In each of the particular localities that I visited a number of individuals were especially helpful: in Cardiff, Sheikh Said, the late Salih Hassan al-Udhaini, Abdullah Mohammad al-Udhaini, Mrs Olive Suleiman; in Birmingham, Muhammad Abdullah Abdulilah; in Sheffield, Abdul Qalil Sha'if, Andy Shallice; in South Shields, Dave Byrne, Abdullah Hassan al-Hukaimi; in London, Hajj Salih Berim. Over many years, the staff of the Yemen embassies in London were most encouraging and forthcoming in response to my inquiries. To all of these people, and to many others who gave time and help, I should like to express my gratitude. I hope they will recognize in this portrait of the Yemeni community they know so well at least some of the insights and information they were kind enough to share with me.

London, July 1991

Britain's First Muslims

Chapter 1

Yemeni Migration and its Contexts

Over the past century or more, people from over a dozen Arab countries have settled in Britain. This flow of Arabs to Britain increased greatly in the 1970s and 1980s with the result that by the end of the 1980s several hundred thousand, perhaps up to half a million people from Arab countries, or of Arab descent, were living in the UK.[1] This is a study of one such Arab community in Britain, that of immigrants from what were, until their unification in May 1990, the distinct states of North and South Yemen. Sharply contrasted in origin and social character from later Arab settlers, these Yemenis are the longest-established of the Arab, and Muslim, communities in Britain.

Before examining the character of Yemeni migration itself this introduction will outline briefly the way in which this process of Yemeni migration to Britain relates to the two wider processes of which it has been a small but revealing part – emigration from Arab countries as a whole, and immigration to Britain over the past century. The flow of Yemenis into Britain has been a tiny part of two much larger streams, the first of which has moved some millions of Arabs to live and work outside their native countries, in the Middle East or beyond, and the second of which has brought up to four million people to Britain on a more or less permanent basis.

Arab Migration: An Overview

To begin with, it is necessary to specify what is meant here by 'Arab' and by 'immigrant community'. An Arab is a citizen of an

Arab League country whose mother-tongue is Arabic. Thus, not only citizens of Arab states but also Palestinians, who have so far been denied statehood but who are entitled to it and are native Arab speakers, should also be included as Arabs. This means that Arabs were found in many countries, twenty-two in total, with a population in the 1980s of over 170 million. These countries were: Morocco, Algeria, Tunisia, Libya, Egypt, Sudan, Palestine, Lebanon, Syria, Iraq, Jordan, Kuwait, Bahrain, Qatar, the Emirates, Saudi Arabia, North Yemen, South Yemen and Oman. In addition to Palestine, Mauritania, with a partly Arab-speaking population, and two other Arab League countries – Djibouti and Somalia – are sometimes included. As we shall see there has been emigration on a regional or international basis from at least ten of these. Apart from the Yemenis, established communites from four of them – Iraq, Egypt, Morocco, Palestine – can be found in Britain, with identifiable resident groups of a less permanent kind from at least another five.

The use of the phrase 'immigrant communities' is designed to indicate that this study focuses on a group of Arabs who have not merely come to Britain for a period of residence, but have also fulfilled two further criteria: (a) they have worked here, as opposed to merely resided; and (b) they have to some extent remained in contact with each other as fellow emigrants from a particular country through residence in a common urban area, work in a similar branch of economic activity and the creation of some kind of communal organization. Here the Yemenis can be contrasted to the majority of other Arabs in Britain who congregated in and around London. London has been a haven for refugees from all over the world since the early nineteenth century, and few of the upheavals in the Arab world can have failed to contribute to the number of political refugees in Britain. The revolution in Egypt in 1952 and in Iraq in 1958, to name but two, certainly did so. In the first decade of this century a group of Egyptian nationalists were active in London in the cause of their national independence. But such individual refugees are not the centre of this study. Nor is the Yemeni community comparable to the much larger flow of Arab tourists, entrepreneurs and refugees who have come to Britain since the beginning of the oil boom: in the 1970s, up to 200,000 or more citizens of Arab countries came to London as tourists in the course of one year, and from the early

1970s onwards a larger number of Arabs established some kind of residence in Britain. By the end of the 1980s it was calculated that up to half a million Arabs lived most or part of the year in Britain. However, despite their numerical superiority and the publicity they received, they did not constitute *immigrants*, for their main country of residence and work remained in the Middle East. Moreover, because for the most part they did not settle here, they cannot be said to constitute a *community* in any proper sense of the word. They came mainly for personal, domestic and leisure reasons, or for business that took them to and from the Middle East.

One further point should be clarified about the use of the term 'Arab' in this study, namely the question of religion. Despite the fact that the majority of Arabs are adherents of Islam, there have always been in the Arab world substantial minorities which are Arab-speaking but profess other religions – notably Judaism and Christianity. Emigration among these non-Muslims has been substantial, for either economic or political reasons, and they have been well represented within the Arab immigrant communities in Britain. The creation of Israel in 1948 and its sequel has driven a wedge between Arab Jews and Arab Muslims, and most Jews no longer regard themselves, nor are so regarded, as Arabs: but this is a relatively recent development, and in earlier periods the Arab community in Britain comprised active members of all three major Middle Eastern religions. On the other hand, there are Muslims and Christians from Arab countries whose first language is not Arabic: the Kurds of Iraq are mainly Muslim, the Assyrians mainly Christian. There have been numerous Kurdish emigrants to Britain, mainly professional people, and there is a community of a few hundred Assyrians concentrated in the Ealing area of West London. But their first language is not Arabic and they are therefore not classifiable as 'Arabs'.

The Arab immigrant flow to Britain has been a part of two wider processes: Arab emigration, and immigration to Britain. There has been Arab emigration since the seventh century – either within the area now peopled by Arabs or outside it – but here we focus on emigration in the past century or so; this is emigration resulting from the growth of modern trade and industry and the development of economies outside and later inside the Middle East that attracted Arabs from their country of birth. There have also been many cases of emigration resulting from direct political factors – Palestine being the most striking case. Four major kinds of Arab emigration can therefore be noted.

1   *Lebanon*

Beginning in the early 1860s, a flood of Lebanese emigrants crossed the seas to work as traders – in North and South America, Australia, West Africa. A few settled in Europe, including a community of a few dozen families in Manchester.[2] According to some estimates for the 1960s, the total number of people from Lebanon and Syria or descended from such emigrants living in Europe and the Americas came to around 1.25 million, or equal to over one-third the number of people resident in Lebanon itself. The civil war that began in 1975 added to this number, sending an estimated further quarter of a million Lebanese out of the country.

2   *The Yemens*

North and South Yemen, among the poorest countries in the Arab world (populations of roughly ten and two million respectively in the 1980s), had been sending people abroad for centuries. Merchants from the Hadramaut in the South are found all over the Indian Ocean. But in modern times two distinct identifiable flows have occurred. The first, beginning in the 1890s, led thousands of Yemenis, mainly from the North, to work on ships stopping at Aden and later to travel via Aden to work in foreign countries – especially the USA and Britain. The second, resulting from the oil boom elsewhere in the peninsula in the 1970s, led hundreds of thousands of Yemenis – 350,000 from the North and 80,000 from the South – to work in Saudi Arabia and Kuwait as manual labourers.[3]

3   *Palestine*

Of the roughly four and a half million Palestinians in the world, approximately half, that is, over two million, have been driven from their homes and are refugees. Of these over a million have lived in UNRWA camps in Jordan, Syria, Lebanon and Gaza, but a substantial diaspora has also taken place as Palestinians have gone to seek work elsewhere. Most have gone to Saudi Arabia, Kuwait and the Gulf states but others have gone further afield – to the USA, West Germany, Latin America and, in much smaller numbers, to Britain.

4   North Africa

From the early 1950s the three former French colonies of Algeria, Tunisia and Morocco sent substantial numbers of unemployed peasants and urban dwellers to Europe, especially France. By 1974 there were about 450,000 Algerians, 175,000 Moroccans and 85,000 Tunisians, exclusive of their families, working in Europe.[4] A separate but related flow was that of Egyptians, leaving their country for similar reasons but in a different direction: the educated Egyptians (doctors, teachers, technicians) tended to go to richer Arab states, such as Libya and the oil states of the Arabian Peninusla, while the poorer manual workers went first predominantly to Libya and later to Iraq and the Gulf states. Some educated Egyptians went to the USA, and a number came to Britain. From the early 1970s North Africans from all four emigrant countries came to Britain. This did not assume the proportions of the flow to France, but it was a small subsection of the increasing flow of immigrants from the Mediterranean to Britain to work in the service sector in and around London. While most of these migrants stayed for short periods, they were definitely *working* in Britain. By the mid 1980s substantial communities of Moroccans and Egyptians in particular were present in London working in services and the professions.

Each of these four waves of Arab emigration was in the main directed towards countries other than Britain. Three of them went to continents other than Europe – the Lebanese to the Americas, the Yemenis and Palestinians to other parts of the Middle East – and the North African emigration was, while coming to Europe, focused on France. But in each case a trickle came to Britain: the Lebanese from the 1860s, the Yemenis from the 1900s, the Palestinians after 1948 and the North Africans in the 1970s and 1980s. Until the 1980s the most substantial communities – in the sense discussed above of groups of working immigrants with a degree of internal cohesion – were the first two. A few hundred Lebanese, Syrians and Moroccans congregated in Manchester in

Table 1   Immigrants in Britain 1966

	Total	% of population
Irish	2,000,000	4.2
West Indian	454,000	1.0
Jewish	410,000	0.9
Indian and Pakistani	359,000	0.8
Polish	130,000	0.3
Cypriot	100,000	0.2

(Source: E. Krausz, *Ethnic Minorities in Britain*)

the 1860s and afterwards. The much more numerous Yemenis, who numbered up to 15,000 at their peak, are the subject of the chapters that follow.

Immigrants in Britain

In contrast to France in particular, these Arab immigrants were relatively insignificant within the overall context of immigration into Britain over the same period. The numbers involved – a few hundred Lebanese and Syrians, a few thousand Yemenis, perhaps a few thousand North Africans and a few hundred Palestinians – were tiny compared to the three to four million immigrants who settled in Britain in modern times. Table 1 depicts the main immigrant communities in Britain according to the 1966 census.

The Irish began immigration into Britain in substantial numbers as a result of the agricultural crisis of the 1840s, the Jews fled from Eastern Europe from the 1880s onwards, and the Poles and other smaller Eastern European groups came before or just after the Second World War. Since the war, large numbers of immigrants from former British colonies also entered the country to work in industry and services. Despite their distinct origins, the different groups of Arab immigrants therefore form part of these larger flows and, on closer examination, can be seen to share many features of them. The Yemenis who settled in the ports did so in company with other colonial sailors – West Indians especially – who had also been recruited to British ships. As will be discussed in Chapter 6, the postwar Yemenis are in several respects very similar to the South Asians who came to work in British industry as, predominantly, unskilled workers. The North

Africans have come like those from the northern Mediterranean countries to work in the service sector, a small transplant of a much wider continental European development on to British conditions. Even the Manchester Arab merchants of the nineteenth century were part of a larger community of foreign merchants who set up home and traded in textiles. Finally, the Palestinians, although driven out by a in some respects unique process of colonization of their land, can be seen as another group of people displaced from their country by recent political upheavals, and in this sense comparable to the Eastern Europeans who fled from fascism or from the postwar communist regimes.

While several comparisons of cause can be made, there are also quantitative analogies: even in numerical terms, the Arabs are not alone at the bottom of the list. The largest groups of immigrants have numbered hundreds of thousands or more: they comprise the Irish, West Indians, South Asians and Jews. There then follows a middle range from 10,000 to 200,000 including the Poles, Italians, Cypriots, Chinese, Maltese and many others. Finally there are even smaller groups, but ones which retain some degree of communal organization around their places of residence and worship. The Georgians and Ukrainians, for example, number a few thousand, and there are no doubt other ethnic groups similarly submerged in the wider immigrant spectrum; Goans, Koreans and Latin American communities among them. These smaller groups are distinct in their countries of origin and in the customs they retain in Britain: yet they share many characteristics with other groups, both in terms of the reasons why they migrated, the general conditions under which they did so, and the manner of their employment within Britain itself.

For this reason one can say that Arab immigration to Britain, and that of Yemenis in particular, is a coincidence on a comparatively small scale of two much larger trends – Arab emigration in general, and modern immigration to Britain. The causes and course of these much wider processes can help to explain why this Arab community lives and works in Britain today.

The Yemeni Background

The growth and character of Yemeni immigration into Britain can be best understood by looking first at its background. There is one brutal unchanging factor behind it: both parts, North and South, were among the poorest countries in the world. In the 1980s the per capita income of those living in North Yemen (after 1962 the Yemeni Arab Republic) and of those in the South (after 1969 the People's Democratic Republic of Yemen) was still below $300 per annum. But beyond this general poverty the development of Yemeni emigration in the past century has many specific features that help to explain its particular character.

Until the unification of May 1990 there were two Yemeni states. At first sight it might seem that this division was of no particular significance: peasants from North and South left their villages for the same economic reason – to find work abroad; and both at home and in exile all Yemenis, while aware of 'tribal' and regional differences, felt themselves to be from one country. The division between North and South had existed since the eighteenth century when a ruler at Lahej outside Aden broke away from the control of the imams in North Yemen. It was further accentuated, first by the fact that Britain ruled the South and not the North, and second by the very divergent social and political upheavals that the two parts of Yemen underwent in the 1960s. But although in the 1960s, 1970s and 1980s there existed a conservative state in the North and a revolutionary state in the South, there also existed a deep sense of a common Yemeni identity and culture, and an unrelenting hope for a unification of the two countries, one shared by most exiles.[5] As one British observer of the Yemeni community in South Shields in the early 1950s discovered, the divisions that English people believed were important were not considered so by Yemenis: 'We are the same people from Yemen and Aden – no differences. Just a line divides our people – one British, the other Yemen – but same people – no differences,' he was told.[6]

In another sense, though, Yemen was neither one nor two, but *four* units, and this division was extremely relevant to Yemeni emigration. First of all, in the eastern part of what was South Yemen lay the area known as the Hadramaut. It consists of a coastal city, Mukalla, and then, over some mountains, the fertile valley of Wadi Hadramaut, where there are a number of towns. The Hadramaut has a long history of emigration, and Hadramis have been traders in the Indian ocean for centuries. Indeed the prosperity of the towns of the interior has depended on this

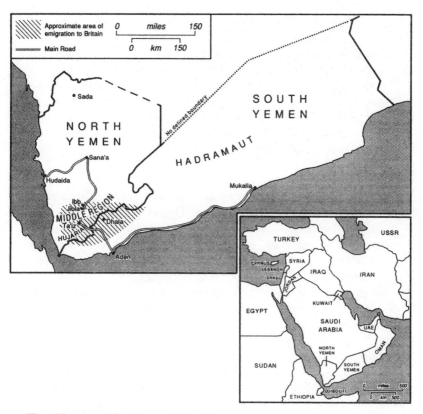

The Yemen: North and South

activity in exile. In the Arab world, too, Hadrami merchants have played a significant role: the famous medieval social thinker Ibn Khaldun, born in Tunis in 1332, was from a Hadrami family, and since the oil-based prosperity began in neighbouring Saudi Arabia Hadrami traders and financiers have prospered there. The largest Hadrami exile community was, however, in Singapore and Java where these Arab traders built up a powerful position under, respectively, British and Dutch colonial rule. As one observer put it:

Emigration was vital to the Hadramis in order to compensate for the difficulty of making a livelihood at home by sending remittances from abroad. Those who went to East Africa rarely made fortunes, those who went to Hyderabad sometimes did rather better, but the wealthiest Hadramis were those who emigrated to Singapore and Java. They not only supported numerous relatives at home in comparative luxury, but indirectly gave work to builders, craftsmen, agricultural labourers, and the beduin who carried thier goods from the coast to the inland towns. ... In 1939 there were about 80,000 Hadramis in the East Indies whose strong ties with their homelands made them follow events there with the greatest attention.[7]

Small Hadrami communities existed not only in India, but also in several East African countries – Uganda, Kenya, Ethiopia, Tanzania. Later the position of the Hadramis was threatened by nationalist feeling in the countries concerned; but most Hadramis were able to continue their activities in South-East Asia and elsewhere, especially in the Arabian oil states.

A second, distinct, area of Yemen is the port of Aden itself. Most of those Yemenis who came to Britain in the century have been referred to as 'Adenis': but this was inaccurate. While it was long common to call everyone from the region 'Adenis', it is important to distinguish between the minority who were Adenis, born and bred, and the majority, peasants who flowed into the area from the South and North Yemeni countryside during the boom of the 1950s. In 1955 35 per cent of the population of Aden – 48,000 people – were North Yemenis and a further 19,000 – 14 per cent of the total – were from the South Yemeni hinterland. Only 37,000, or 27 per cent, were strictly speaking Adenis. Moreover, after the economy of Aden was undermined in 1967 by the closure of the Suez Canal, most of those who had migrated to the port left again, back to the countryside or to the oil-producing states. Those Adenis, in the strict sense, who left tended to move either to North Yemen, where they continued their traditional importing activities, or to the oil states of the Gulf.

Most of the population of Yemen live in the mountains that stretch north from Aden to the Hijaz area of Saudi Arabia. Here the majority of the population are peasants, many of whom own a bit of land, but most of whom have to work, or had to work, as sharecroppers on the land of richer proprietors. Within this peasant community, there existed tribal divisions and on top of these a strong religious division, between those who were followers of the Zeidi branch of Islam and those who were Shafeis.[8] The theological difference between these two is not relevant here; what is pertinent is the fact that, until the late 1970s, virtually all Yemeni emigration was from the Shafei areas alone. These Shafei areas straddled the division between the two Yemeni states: the area north of Aden, and the southern part of North Yemen were both Shafei. The Yemenis themselves refer to the Shafei areas of the North, quite accurately, as 'the middle region' (*al-mantaqa al-'usta*) and it is this area, around Ta'iz and towns such as Rada, Ibb and Zabid, which has produced the greatest flow of emigrants.

Apparently cut off as these areas were from the outside world they were none the less linked by a set of factors promoting migration. All labour migration, like inflation, is a mixture of 'push' and 'pull' factors, of both supply and demand; and beyond the absolute fact of poverty it is possible to identify certain specific 'push' and 'pull' elements. Although very poor for centuries, North Yemen became poorer in the twentieth century under the rule of the imams. Yemen's main export, coffee, declined and the imams penalized trade and discouraged any attempts at business activities. This conservative policy was particularly felt in the Shafei areas, since the imams were Zeidis and favoured the followers of their own sect. The discrimination against the Shafei areas was especially fierce after 1948, when the imams crushed an attempt by merchants and other liberal reformers in the Shafei area to overthrow their regime. Although the imams were overthrown in 1962 this was followed by eight years of civil war in which an estimated 250,000 people died; subsequently the North Yemeni economy was heavily reliant on workers' remittances and on foreign aid. In South Yemen the Shafei areas were, until 1967, ruled by sultans and sheikhs backed by Britain and here too there was a stagnating economic situation. Although Aden boomed, the Yemeni countryside did not; in order to insulate the sultans from political pressures, no attempt was made to link the evolution of the two. Even the food required by Aden was brought from abroad – meat from Somalia and vegetables down the Red Sea from Lebanon and Cyprus. Under-employment and stagnation, in part the product of political factors, therefore characterized the Shafei areas of both North and South Yemen, and impelled many of the young men of the villages into exile. It is indicative of the social relations prevailing in the rural areas that elder sons tended not to migrate: those who left were the second or third sons, those who might in the past have inherited some land but who in more difficult circumstances did not.

On the 'pull' side there were a number of different factors. The first modern demand came from the British Merchant Navy, which around 1900 began hiring engine-room crews in colonial ports – in the West Indies, West Africa, Singapore, Hong Kong and Aden. These were hired through middlemen who, in the Yemeni case, had offices at Steamer Point, the centre of Aden port. Crews were usually brought on in groups of sixteen: twelve firemen, three greasers, who as their name implies cleaned and oiled the engines, and one donkeyman, responsible for the 'donkey-engine' which fed the boiler. The Mechant Navy made a point of hiring a crew all from the same tribal grouping: the practice was for these below-deck crews to be Yemenis, Africans or Chinese, and for the on-deck crew to be British. As a result of this policy, Yemeni peasants became global sailors, and small colonies of Yemenis grew up in ports visited by ships from Aden – in Marseilles, Le Havre, New York, Rotterdam and in some of the coastal cities of Britain. It is from these Yemeni sailors, who continued coming till after the Second World War, that the first Yemeni communities in Britain were drawn.

A second demand came after the Second World War, both on the doorstep of the Shafei mountains and further afield. Aden itself was undergoing a boom – developing an oil refinery and becoming the centre of British military operations in the Middle East. Commercial and construction activity attracted thousands of workers, and some at least of these went on to emigrate to Britain. They were drawn to the UK by the demand for unskilled and semi-skilled labour which attracted hundreds of thousands of immigrants from the West Indies and South Asia to Britain, and which attracted millions of other workers from southern Europe and North Africa to Western Europe. The Yemenis formed a small fraction of this flow into Britain, but they went into the same kind of jobs as the larger numbers of Jamaicans and Pakistanis or, in continental Western Europe, Algerians and Turks. To sum up: three factors combined to produce this wave of Yemeni emigration – the boom in Aden, the demand in the industrialized countries of Europe, and, not to be forgotten, the deterioration of conditions in the Shafei areas of the North after the defeat of the 1948 revolt.

A third kind of demand for Yemeni labour, and by far the largest, came with the boom in the oil-producing states of the Gulf. Oil itself employs relatively few people: in larger Gulf states, at most 1–2 per cent of the labour-force finds work in that branch of economic activity which provides the majority of government revenue and well over 90 per cent of foreign exchange. In those countries with relatively large populations, such as Iran and Algeria, the oil boom coincided with continued under-employment of the labour-force, and as a result Algerian workers continued to flow to France and Iranian workers to Kuwait and Dubai. In the oil states of the Peninsula there is very little available manpower, and in all of these there was a net import of labour: this went not into the oil sector directly, but into branches of economic activity that had grown with the rise in oil revenues. Construction, trade, government service all boomed; to a lesser extent there was also a growth in industrial employment. In the 1960s and 1970s North and South Yemen provided much of this labour: if the Arabian Peninsula is seen as one economic and demographic unit, the Yemeni peasantry formed the nearest available source of rural labour to be attracted into the urban-developing sector. This of course further accentuated the imbalance between the backward countryside and the areas undergoing an oil boom since no coherent measures were taken to invest profits from the oil sector in the agricultural regions. As a result more emigration and further imbalance followed.

In the 1980s, and until their mass expulsion at the time of the Gulf crisis in August 1990, as many as one million people from North and South Yemen, first generation migrants or descendants, were working in Saudi Arabia, where the total Saudi population was probably not more than 6 million. The longer-established ones were in business and services, but the main field of activity of the first generation migrants was in construction and other unskilled labouring jobs; despite its enormous wealth Saudi Arabia had created little manufacturing industry. Industrial development tended to be petrochemicals or steel plants. More-over, in most cases, South Asian and Far Eastern construction firms brought in their own labour forces. Industry therefore did not provide a source of employment for Yemenis, and nor did the state apparatus: employment in the burgeoning army was reserved for Saudi Arabian beduin. By the late 1970s an estimated 80,000 South Yemenis had also gone to work in Saudi Arabia: a small percentage were political refugees who fled in or after 1967, but the majority were, as with those from North Yemen, merely in search of a job. There were tens of thousands of Yemenis working in unskilled jobs in Kuwait. Until it became independent in 1977 there were also an estimated 15,000 from North and South in the French colony of Djibouti (total population 150,000).

Small groups of Yemenis could be found in other Middle Eastern states, but outside the Arab world the two largest communities were in the USA and Britain. In the former there had been colonies of Yemeni sailors since the 1900s, and in the 1970s and 1980s a community of Yemenis developed in New York. But the two largest groupings were of more recent origin. One was in the South Dearborn area of Detroit, where Yemenis made up around 1000 of the 4000 or so Arabs living there in the 1970s. The main form of employment was in the nearby Rouge motor plant of the Ford motor company. The other concentration of Yemenis was in California, where they had worked on a seasonal basis as fruit pickers. Precise figures are not available, but one estimate suggests that over the 1970s as many as 100,000 Yemenis came to work for a period in the California fields.[9] In that period, they were reckoned to send home $1000 to $1500 a year and were often living in atrocious barracks. They also became involved in clashes over unionization of farm labour: in 1973 a Yemeni labour organizer, Naji Daifullah, was killed by a local sheriff during a clash with the police over a strike.

'The Disaster of the Twentieth Century'

The extent of this Yemeni emigration has surpassed that of any other country in the Middle East in recent times: even Lebanon has exported less labour than North and South Yemen, and Lebanese emigrants were able to achieve a more prosperous existence than the Yemenis. For the area left behind, this emigration has also meant high costs. In the first place there is the dreadful emotional cost to the workers and their families of separation for years on end. It is not difficult to read on the faces of Yemeni workers a deep sadness born of years of emotional restriction and harshness: if one could see the faces of the women and children left behind in the villages of 'the middle region' there would no doubt be the same melancholy. The pain of emigration, and the sadness it occasions at home, are a recurring theme in Yemeni poetry.

Second, labour emigration of this kind represents a misallocation of resources. If the human skills and energy used to gain a wage outside Yemen were deployed inside, the country would benefit greatly. But while there exists a substantial Yemeni industrial work-force outside North and South Yemen, there is far less industrial employment inside. The contributions which these workers make to the domestic economy is via remittances; but while these pay for consumer goods the evaluative question is how far the remittances enable their country to redress the imbalance between itself and the outside world, to lessen the gap between itself and the countries which absorb its labour. In many cases, the injection of foreign currency is used to pay for the import of consumer goods, and in this situation no restoration of the balance is taking place. In fact a new dependence is created, in that the economy of villages whose men are working abroad becomes tied to the flow, and when remittances decline or cease the village loses its lifeline. A good example of this was the Hadramaut, where there was famine during the Second World War after the Japanese invasion of the East Indies cut off the flow of money from merchants there. North Yemen is a good example of a country which faces this problem: with an import bill ten to fifteen times higher than its exports, it was tied to the remittances of its emigrants. In the words of the Minister of Economics in 1975:

Few nations are as dependent as we are on abroad for their development, but what enables us to survive, while waiting for our agriculture to revive and perhaps for some happy surprises from beneath our earth, are our emigrants. From Chicago to Kuwait, from Marseilles to Jeddah they are 1,235,000, and each one sends us, on average, about $1 a day.[10]

A significant proportion of all able-bodied men were therefore working abroad. No wonder that as long ago as 1952 a Yemeni nationalist, writing in Aden, should have commented sadly on this phenomenon: 'The Yemeni case is the disaster of the twentieth century and the real refugee of our times is the Yemeni.'[11]

Chapter 2

The First Yemeni Migration: The Ports

In Yemeni discussions of their community in Britain a *selective geography* is evident: certain towns are known because there are Yemenis there, while others are almost wholly ignored. Although London was always a major port and attracted about half of all post-1945 immigrants, there was only a very small Yemeni settlement there. As far as the earlier, sailor, communities are concerned, the names that crop up again and again are those to which the coal-burning ships from the East seem to have gone – Cardiff, Liverpool, South Shields, Hull. Of these Cardiff, the capital city of Wales or *Bilad al-Welsh* (Land of the Welsh), is the most important.

Cardiff: Tiger Bay and *Bilad al-Welsh*

Cardiff owes its prosperity to the growth of the docks in the nineteenth century: in essence, it was an outlet for coal that was brought down from the valleys of South Wales. In 1801 it had a population of only about 1000, in 1838 it had grown to 10,000, by 1938 it had reached 228,000 and by 1966 291,000. The great majority of those who came to Cardiff were from Wales and England, but from the 1880s onwards a small community of foreign sailors began to settle in the area known as Butetown. This was a district of about 1 square mile in size, built on land reclaimed from the sea by the Second Marquis of Bute earlier in the nineteenth century. Although originally inhabited by ships' captains and other middle-class people, it gradually became the place where foreign seamen stayed while in Cardiff. By 1900 there were West Indian, West African, Chinese and Yemenis living in this area; and during the First World War the demand for such crews increased further, so that in 1919, there were reckoned to be around 1200 unemployed 'coloured' sailors in Cardiff.[1]

Butetown was, and to some extent still is, a ghetto – an area defined socially and geographically by the rest of the community, in this case Cardiff, as being separate and reserved for an alien grouping. The Butetown area before the First World War acquired an exotic reputation and was often referred to as 'Tiger Bay', a term used both about the whole district and about its centre, Loudoun Square. An indication of how others regarded it is to be found in the following quotation from a Welsh novelist:

> There was fascination in the walk through Tiger Bay. Chinks and Dagoes, Lascars and Levantines slippered about the faintly evil by-ways that ran off Bute Street. . . . The flags of all nations fluttered on the house fronts, and ever and anon the long bellowing moan of a ship coming to the docks or outward bound seemed the very voice of this meeting place of the seven seas. It was a dirty, rotten and romantic district, an offence and an inspiration, and I loved it.[2]

This is a revealing quotation for two reasons: first, because it evokes the *mixture* of attraction and prejudice that made up the popular myth of Tiger Bay; second, because it illustrates one way in which Arabs and Yemenis were invisible because they were reclassified in a more romantic way. 'Lascars' and 'Levantines' were common late nineteenth-century terms. 'Lascar', ultimately derived from the Arabic word *askari* meaning soldier, had entered Anglo-Indian parlance from Urdu; first it meant an Indian soldier, and later became the normal term for South Asian and so Yemeni crewmen.[3] 'Levantine' referred indiscriminately to the inhabitants of the Ottoman Empire, often also generically referred to as 'Turks'. It included Greeks, Turks, Arabs, Armenians and Jews, with the faint suggestion of their being somehow mysterious and strange.

Another reason for Butetown's ghetto character was its physical isolation. Butetown was and is cut off from the rest of Cardiff. In the early period, it was bounded on the south by the docks and the sea, on the west by the Glamorgan Canal (now filled in), on the east by more docks, and on the north by a railway line. There is only one proper entrance, under the railway bridge and down Bute Street. Migrant communities in Butetown had little reason to go into Cardiff, while inhabitants of, or visitors to, Cardiff had no reason to go to Butetown, and many seem to have believed that they would be robbed or stabbed if they went there after dark. The only exception to this isolation was during the big rugby matches at Cardiff Arms Park, less than ten minutes' walk from the entrance to Bute Street. During the matches, thousands of young men would come down from the valleys for the afternoon and then go on to drink in the pubs which ran along part of Bute Street.

Inside Butetown itself, the visiting sailors at first lived in lodging houses. These were run by sailors for men of their own nationality. A Yemeni or a West Indian arriving in Cardiff would go to one of these houses, and find there a bed, and food, news from home and people whom he could talk to. Sailors used to leave their valuables with the lodging-house keeper, and the latter would often be responsible for finding a sailor another ship to sign on with. As time went by, however, this transitory form of existence gave way to a more settled community. Sailors tended to return again and again to Cardiff and treat it as a home: they got together to buy cheap houses, and some began to get jobs in the docks rather than on ocean-going ships. Moreover, a considerable number set up house with Welsh women who had come from the valleys, and in time a generation of part Welsh and part Yemeni or West Indian origin was born.

No precise figures on the number of foreign seamen and their families exist, but the total community in Butetown in the first part of the twentieth century was around 5000 and of these the majority were foreign sailors or their descendants. One survey of a school in the area, carried out in the 1940s, found that while only 25 per cent of the children's fathers were British-born, 81 per cent of their mothers were. Fourteen per cent of the fathers were classified as Arabs. There are some figures on the numbers of sailors employed on Cardiff ships and these give a rough indication of the numbers employed: in 1934, when there were 2460 coloured 'alien' seamen registered in Cardiff, 993 were Arabs, another 232 Somalis, 328 West Indians, 372 Africans and 135 Indians. Arabs, virtually all of whom must have been Yemenis and Somalis, together therefore made up nearly half of all the

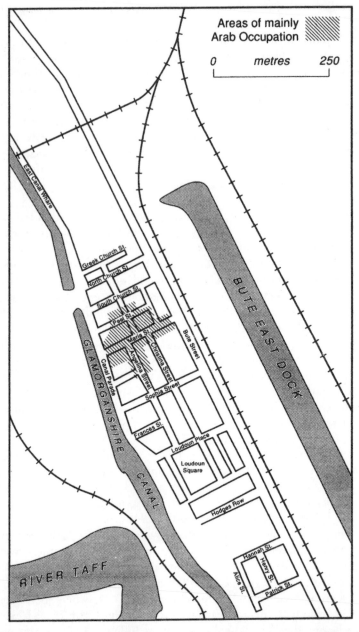

Butetown in the 1940s (source: K. S. Little, *Negroes in Britain*)

Table 2   Lascars as Percentage of Those Employed on British Ships

1911	12.3
1921	29.1
1930	27.1
1931	29.0
1936	24.2

Source: Little, *Negroes in Britain,* p. 72.

seamen registered. Although the absolute numbers declined later in the decade, the proportions remained the same. Overall figures for the number of 'lascars' (only a small proportion of whom were Yemenis) employed on British ships show that from before the First World War until a bit before the Second they formed a substantial part of the total (see Table 2).

The Second World War led to a rise in demand for foreign seamen, as had the First, and in 1942 a register of foreign seamen revealed the following percentages in Cardiff:[4]

Arabs	30 per cent
Somalis	20 per cent
Africans	22 per cent
West Indians	6 per cent
Malays, Indians, Portuguese and others	32 per cent

Assuming that about 5000–6000 people were referred to, this would mean there were 1500 Yemenis and 1000 Somalis in Cardiff during the Second World War. Their relatively larger proportions are confirmed by figures on the number of lodging houses and beds by different nationalities available in the mid 1920s and mid 1940s. In 1926 there were twenty-two 'Arab', presumably Yemeni, boarding houses and three Arab–Egyptian out of a total of 109.[5] Figures for the 1940s show that out of a total of around fifty such houses, seventeen were classed as 'Arab', with 186 beds in all, and another four as 'Somali', with twenty-eight beds in all. The majority of the Yemenis and Somalis would by then have been living in homes and no longer in lodging houses; but the proportions available bear out the position of the Yemenis and Somalis in the community as a whole.

Crew register of the *Italiana*, dated Cardiff, 25 May 1916. Crewmen numbers 16–20 have Yemeni names, give Aden as nationality, and addresses at Bute Street and Maria Street in Butetown (*Courtesy Welsh Industrial and Maritime Museum, Cardiff*)

The 1940s represented the high point in the development of Butetown as a cosmopolitan community of sailors and their families, and this was especially true for the Yemenis and Somalis. There are at least three reasons for this. In the first place Cardiff declined as a maritime centre after the Second World War: in 1920 there were 380 vessels registered in Cardiff, whereas by 1969 there were only twenty-one. Coal-burning ships gave way to oil-burners, and other ports such as Port Talbot opened up in South Wales. As a result the numbers of foreign sailors coming to Cardiff declined, and the pattern of employment changed.

Table 3   Butetown Employment in 1966

	Males	Females
Manufacturing, construction		
Gas, electric, water	1910	590
Transport	530	110
Distribution and civilian services	740	990
National and local government	15	9
Other	185	91
Total	3380	1790

Source: Little, p. 20.

Whereas in the 1940s nearly all the men in Butetown were working on the sea, this fell off in the following two decades, and at the same time the women began to take paid employment, whereas previously they had been confined to housework.

Because of the depression of Cardiff relative to the rest of the United Kingdom, comparatively few immigrants of the post-1945 period came there: in 1967 it was estimated that there were only about 8000 non-white people in Cardiff, 3 per cent of the total population, with another 1000 in Newport.

A second change which further reduced the influx of Arabs was that Yemenis stopped going to sea on British ships. This was not due to a decline of the overall numbers of 'lascars' or, as they are now called, 'Asian seamen'. As late as 1976 an estimated 22,000 Asians served with around 40,000 British seamen in the Merchant Navy. Most of these were, however, from India, Pakistan and Bangladesh. Why the proportion of Yemenis should have declined so much is not clear: it may have been due to a change in Merchant Navy employment policy, but a contributing factor must have been that other more lucrative and less arduous forms of employment were now available to the impoverished peasants of Dhala and the Shafei 'middle region'. They could now work in Aden or in the factories of the British Midlands. In the latter a Yemeni worker can earn £3000 a year or more, while in 1976 an Asian seaman was getting £500 – one-sixth of the wages received by his English counterpart above decks. Whatever the reasons for this decline, there was a falling off in the numbers of Yemeni seamen coming to Britain after the Second World War; although some continued to come to Cardiff they tended to be individuals with relatives or with friends there to receive them.

A third factor that drew a line between the two periods was the redevelopment of Butetown itself in the late 1960s, at a cost of £2.5 million. For behind the exotic image of Tiger Bay lay poverty and deprived conditions: the tuberculosis rate there was seven times the national average in 1951, and housing conditions there were appalling. In the 1960s Cardiff City Council therefore pulled down the old rows of terraced houses, and many streets were completely removed. None of the old cafés or boarding houses remained, and those living in the area were offered the opportunity to settle elsewhere in Cardiff. Most of the inhabitants did not, however, leave; lamenting the death of the old community, they preferred to live in their area. The Yemenis and Somalis, known among the others as rather 'clannish' and 'keeping to themselves', nearly all stayed in the new Butetown. They were near their mosques, and near each other.

The 1919 Riots

The Arab community in Cardiff has undergone two major trials in the past seventy or eighty years. The first of these was the violent racialist attack to which they, like other immigrants, were subjected in 1919. The outbreak that occurred in the summer of 1919 was not confined to Cardiff: similar events were reported in Liverpool, South Shields, London and Hull. In Cardiff, however, the rioting was for the repatriation of the non-white sailors to their home countries. An underlying factor was unemployment after the war, but it is evident that this only brought into the open a hostility that already existed among the white community.

The Welsh riots began on the night of Saturday 7 June 1919 in the nearby town of Newport and spread to Cardiff and Barry on the night of Wednesday 11 June. A crowd of around 2000 people gathered outside the Labour Exchange offices in Cardiff's Canal Parade and began attacking non-white seamen. They then attacked a number of house-fronts in Bute Street, shouting 'Fetch them out' and 'Kill them'. The local paper later carried a picture of an Arab lodging house that had been wrecked by a mob.

Another victim was a local Islamic leader. In the words of the local paper:

> Hadji Mahomet, the Somali priest, was reported to be living at 1, Homfray Street, and the rioters visited him. In response to the entreaties of his white wife to leave for a place of safety he clambered up a drainpipe at the back of his house. He was immune from the fury of the crowd while hidden on the roof, and with true Eastern stoicism watched his residence being reduced to a skeleton. Every window in the house was broken, and matters looked decidedly ugly when extra police arrived.[6]

A number of shots were fired in these riots; in all fifteen people were reported to have been seriously injured, and one white man was killed. Following these riots six people were charged in court, but while only one was an Englishman, four were Arabs and the sixth a man named Elmi Herse (probably a Somali name). The four Arabs arrested were named as: Ali Abdul, twenty-four years old, charged with shooting at people; Mohamed Khaid, twenty-five, charged with shooting at a policeman; Mohomed Abouki, forty, charged with assaulting a constable; Hassan Ali, twenty-two, charged with the same. Later, on Friday 12 June, more people were charged in connection with the riots, among them five Arabs. One, John Abdulla, aged thirty-seven, ran a lodging house at 57 Millicent Street and was accused of firing shots. The sentences passed on those arrested included sentences of hard labour from two to six months.

Further riots were reported two nights later, as described in the local paper:

> There were many brave spirits well out of the danger zone. They had allotted to themselves the task of cheering the invaders and accepting the booty as it was handed out. Old women and slatternly young women shrieked encouragement, and it was a sight reminiscent of the French Revolution.[7]

Five people were reported seriously injured, among them three Arabs:

> Ali Abdul, an Arab residing at 250, Butestreet, scalp wounds and abdominal injuries.

> Mohamed Hassan, an Arab, 14 Loudoun Square, Cardiff, fractured skull.
>
> An Arab, name not known, fractured skull.

The third, unnamed man, was in fact called Mahomet Abdullah, and he died of his wounds a day later. No more serious riots followed after those outbreaks: on the night after the one in which Mahomet Abdullah and his fellow Arabs were injured, the police were present in force, and arrested an ex-soldier who was charged with being drunk and with chasing an Arab through the streets. But the community, Arab, West Indian and Chinese, remained at home for days after, hiding indoors with the windows barred. Years later the people of the area still remembered these incidents with fear.

A surprising feature of the riots is the apparent prominence of Arab names among those residents of Butetown who were caught up in clashes, presumably defending their homes or fighting back. While Arabs made up only 20 per cent of the population at this time, most of the arrested and injured had Arab names, and the one resident to die was also an Arab. No obvious reason for this imbalance suggests itself: the most likely explanation is that it was the Arabs who found their jobs most threatened. Another feature of the riots is the manner in which it illustrated the presence of a racist opinion within the population. The combination of prejudices can be gauged from the following account given after the first riots in Newport:

> There is much comment in the town as to the real cause of the disturbances. There are those who openly allege that a number of Sinn Feiners and Bolsheviks who have come to the town and district during the war are behind the trouble. Speaking to a group of workmen on Saturday night one heard the following: 'We went to war and these blackmen and foreigners came here and took our jobs and many businesses. Now we can't get our jobs back and we can't get a house to live in'.[8]

While this was a spontaneous reaction, the response of one local trade union branch was not much better: on 16 June the Cardiff (No. 7) branch of the National Union of Railwaymen passed a motion which, after expressing concern at the situation in the ports, called on the government 'to do their duty by the coloured men in this country and send them back to their homeland'.[9]

These attitudes found a favourable echo in the local paper, the *Western Mail*. In an editorial on 13 June it urged repatriation of negroes 'even under some measure of compulsion'. 'The Arabs', it added, 'are mainly seamen and their repatriation should be a simpler matter'. It went on to attack inter-racial sexual relations and even implicitly condoned the practice of lynching:

In the United States the force of public concern, reinforced by unofficial public action of a ruthless kind, is sufficient to prevent the mischief. In our own country the tolerance which is exhibited towards the problem is due not to far-fetched ideas of racial equality, but to slackness. Such consorting is necessarily an illconsorting; it exhibits either a state of depravity or a squalid infatuation; it is repugnant to all our finer instincts in which pride of race occupied a just and inevitable place, and it produces a state of violent resentment on part of the relations of the misguided girls and women.

The 1919 riots were the worst in Butetown's history, but others followed, and racist ideas continued to be evident in less dramatic ways through discriminatory practices. One result of the riots after the First World War was the enactment of legislation by the government cutting down the employment of non-white seamen through the passing of the 1923 Aliens Act, one in a long line of such restrictive measures. During the 1930s British sailors pressed the government and the shipping industry not to hire non-British labour and, as already mentioned, the hiring of Asian seamen at 20 per cent of the British sailor's wages continued into the 1970s and beyond.

Sheikh Abdullah Ali al-Hakimi

A quite different crisis arose for the Yemeni and Somali community after the Second World War: this was not a result of conflicts in Britain, but was related to the development of the liberal opposition in North Yemen and to the attempted revolt of

1948. The central figure in this crisis was Sheikh Abdullah Ali al-Hakimi, a man of considerable energy and organizational ability whose name is still remembered, amid controversy, throughout the Yemeni community in Britain. Although not a great deal is known about him, the outlines of his life and work are relatively clear, as there is some documentation as well as the memories of those who knew him. Al-Hakimi came originally from the Hujairiah area of the 'middle region' and, before his arrival in Britain in 1936, he had worked as a sailor. He had also been to Algeria and had there become the disciple of the founder of a Sufi (mystical Muslim) sect, known as the Allawi Shadhlili sect. This had been established by a Sheikh Ahmad bin Mustapha al-Alawi, who died in 1937 at the town of Mustaganem near Oran.[10] Sheikh Ahmad had appointed al-Hakimi to be the successor in his order and the bearer of the continuity of the sect. Thereafter, al-Hakimi seems to have spent some time with the small Yemeni community in Rotterdam; he then went, briefly, to Cardiff and it was from there that he reached South Shields, home of the largest British community of Yemenis outside Cardiff, in November 1936.

Before al-Hakimi's arrival there were already instances of community organization. In South Shields a Western Islamic Association was established in 1930 by a Somali resident, Khalid Sheldrake, and it tried to raise funds for a mosque. Al-Hakimi was, however, the first person who tried to organize the Yemeni community in Britain as a whole: the manner of his organizing is interesting both because of the specific brand of reforming Islam which he tried to implement, and because of his combination of religious and political organization within the Allawi Society which he founded. As a Muslim sheikh, his first activity was to promote various religious activities; these included prayer five times a day, observance of Ramadan, celebration of the Eid festival, reading of the Koran and the teaching of Arabic. He set aside a room in a house in South Shields which served as a *zawiya*, a social and religious meeting place for followers of the Allawi doctrine.[11] But al-Hakimi was also a modernizer, and he appears to have encouraged his followers to break with some of the ideas and practices traditionally upheld in Muslim countries, North and South Yemen included. In particular, he tried to counter the traditional neglect of women in Islamic education and he made a

Images of the conflict in Yemen, from the Free Yemeni press.

Above: Sheikh Abdullah al-Hakimi (left) confronting the tyrannical Iman Ahmad with the Koran.

Right: a Free Yemeni opponent of the Imams being tortured under the heading 'Who is responsible for this?'.

special effort to teach Islam to the British wives of Yemeni and Somali sailors in South Shields. Secondly, as a result of his observations of life in Britain, he began to stress the importance of a more open attitude to other religions and to emphasize how Muslims could learn from societies and beliefs other than their own. He also began to support the liberal opposition in North Yemen and in the late 1940s he tried to mobilize support among the Yemeni community in Britain for this cause.

In the first two years of his stay in Britain, from 1936 to 1938, al-Hakimi appears to have concentrated his activities in South Shields. There he collected money for a mosque – a plan that did not come to fruition – and he organized religious and educational activities in the *zawiya*. But from the start al-Hakimi's attempt to include women in the religious services of the Allawi Society met with opposition. In the words of one account:

> The English wives of Moslems responded enthusiastically to the Sheikh's leadership. Weekly classes for religious instruction were held in the Zoaia [i.e. *zawiya*], in which he was assisted by two local female proselytes whom he had trained for that purpose.
>
> These meetings were regularly attended by the women. Marriages were celebrated by the Sheikh according to the Moslem rite, and the women learned to prepare the dead for the funeral ceremony. They requested the burial of women in the Moslem section of the cemetery. The attitude of the Sheikh towards women with regard to the Moslem religion was a deviation from the normal pattern to which the immigrants were accustomed. Consequently, they reacted unfavourably to this departure, opposing the practice of women having a room in the Zoaia for their religious meetings. Ultimately, the women were deprived of this room and along with it the privilege of holding their meetings, and if there were prospects of a restoration of these privileges, hopes faded with the departure of the Sheikh to Cardiff.[12]

Al-Hakimi left South Shields for the larger community at Cardiff in 1938, whether because of setbacks encountered in the former town or not, we do not know. His arrival in Cardiff was reported in the local press.

Sheik Abdulla Ali, a leader of the Moslem faith in Britain, has arrived in Cardiff to direct a scheme for the erection of a mosque. He was met by Sheik Hassan Esmil, and later presided at the Arabs' feast, which is held before the midnight service. Surrounded by his bearded disciples, who sat in a circle attired in their native costume, with bare feet, upon a crimson carpet, Sheik Abdulla Ali told a *Western Mail* representative that he intended to stay in Cardiff for some time.

'It is my ambition to found a mosque in Cardiff, and I shall remain here with my wife, until my ambition has been realised', he said. 'In this city alone there are 5,000 members of our faith, and the only place in which they can worship at present is a room at the premises occupied by the Zaouia Allawia Friendship Society in Bute Street. Of course, the Arab population in Cardiff is a shifting one for many of the Arabs spend the greater part of their time at sea. Those residing in Cardiff, however, meet for prayer five times a day.'[13]

Al-Hakimi's movements over the next few years are obscure. He seems to have started collecting money for his mosque, and he corresponded with the governor of Aden, Sir Bernard Reilly, and others about financial support (see Appendix 1). But some time before the start of the Second World War he went back to North Yemen and he may have stayed there until the war was over. It is known that he visited Ta'iz in 1943, where he collaborated with the Free Yemeni Movement. The mosque project, however, went ahead and was, after some reluctance, patronized by the Colonial Office which was trying to mobilize support for the war effort among colonial peoples. As a result a mosque was opened in 1944: known as the Nur al-Islam mosque it was constructed at the cost of £7000. When al-Hakimi settled in Cardiff again after the war he therefore had his mosque, and in the same building, at 16 Peel Street, he set up an Arabic printing press. On this he began what must by any standards be a striking venture – the publication of a fortnightly paper in Arabic, *al-Salam*, which was almost certainly the first such paper to be produced in Britain. It was also one of the first papers to be produced regularly by Yemenis anywhere, since no press was allowed in North Yemen and the Aden press was still in its infancy. On the same machines al-Hakimi also produced a book entitled *The Religion of God is*

One [Din Allahi Wahid], in which he called for the reform of Islam and the unification of all religions. He said that 500 copies had been produced. Of this book he later wrote:

> In it, to the best of my knowledge, I endeavoured to bring closer together the religious Moslems and Christians, and others, but as regards Religion, God's Religion is one. For those of the past age, and those of this present age, and on the tongues of all the Prophets, was one religion and no other.[14]

The central theme of al-Hakimi's later period was, however, political and involved his support for the 1948 revolt in North Yemen. He seems to have linked up with the Free Yemeni liberal opposition during his return to North Yemen and once *al-Salam* began appearing he used it to reproduce criticisms of the regime in the North. In an open letter to the imam he wrote:

> It is not fair, your Majesty, that the Royal family should be living a very happy life while thousands of your subjects are perishing of hunger. You do not know that the authorities under you are not acting as responsible authorities but as businessmen, selling and buying the subjects of the country? Yemen is an agricultural country and very rich and could support about ten million if there was a responsible administration who could run the subjects and country in a modern way. But the poor Yemeni had become so hungry in his country that he must leave Yemen and go to other foreign country to earn his living.[15]

This policy of opposition to the imam seems to have met with considerable opposition from within the Cardiff community, just as his policy towards women was opposed in South Shields. Several factors seem to have played a role in this. In the first place, many in the community in Cardiff retained strong loyalty to traditional Yemeni and Muslim ideas. They were apparently influenced by the Islamic idea that the imam was both a religious and a secular leader and it was in normal circumstances irreligious to criticize him. Like most exiles they lived a permanent contradiction: they held a romantic idea of how prosperous their country was, even though the only reason they were in exile was that the economic conditions at home had forced them to emigrate. Moreover, by living abroad, they had become out of touch with developments at home: they were therefore immune to the reformist movement that might have affected them had they been at home. The reformers were also drawn from urban, educated sectors, different from the peasant background of the migrants. It took years for the Cardiff community to react to the brutal policies of Imam Ahmad in the Shafei areas of the 'middle region' after 1948. Precisely because they were abroad they had a *more* traditional outlook than many who were at home.

Al-Hakimi, who was both an observant and a curious person, and who *had* been involved in events back in North Yemen, consequently cut himself off from the Cardiff community by attempting to win support for the Free Yemenis. One person who knew him at the time, and who lived through this period in Cardiff, also remarked to me that al-Hakimi was a sincere person 'but he was no politician', and did not know how to counter the opposition of the Yemenis there. The leader of the group against al-Hakimi was Sheikh Hassan Ismail, his former deputy in the Allawi Society. Hassan Ismail upheld the view that all Yemeni Muslims owed loyalty to the imam and that the sheikh should not meddle in politics. Hassan Ismail also had an advantage over al-Hakimi: he had been in Cardiff longer and more consistently than al-Hakimi, and during the Second World War he had acquired a special reputation when a group of people praying with him in the basement of a dwelling in Bute Street were unharmed after a bomb fell on the house. A further factor that may have played an important role was that Hassan Ismail came from the Shamiri district of North Yemen, and the Shamiris were the dominant group in Cardiff. It seems that all the Shamiris followed Hassan Ismail, as did the majority of the Yemeni community, while the Somali community and a minority of non-Shamiri Yemenis sided with al-Hakimi.

The conflict between the two groups, which had begun in 1949, dragged on for some time. Some attempt was made by the followers of Hassan Ismail to oust al-Hakimi from the Nur al-Islam mosque, and on one occasion, in February 1951, there was a meeting of 500 people at which officials from the Islamic Cultural Centre in London tried to settle the disagreement. At various times the Cardiff police were called to the Nur al-Islam mosque when there seemed to be some possibility of a clash between followers of the two leaders. But in the end Hassan Ismail withdrew his followers and they set up a separate centre, a *zawiya* in a private house. Throughout the dispute al-Hakimi continued to produce *al-Salam* and to lay plans for the opening of a school for Muslim children. He raised money in Cardiff and toured other Arab communities to raise his total of £35,000. In 1952, however, he left Cardiff for the Middle East, never to return.

In the last issue of *al-Salam* (no. 107 of 25 May 1952) al-Hakimi printed an article in English thanking the British people for their kindness during his stay and declaring his intention to start producing his paper again in the Middle East. Inside was an article on the achievements of the Allawi Society under al-Hakimi's leadership by a Dr Mohammad Fahmi Mohammad Awadh. It began by praising al-Hakimi's work in spreading Islamic education among the communities in Cardiff, South Shields, Hull, Liverpool and elsewhere. It then went on to list the major aims of the society:

1. Teaching the Qoran to the sons of Moslems, and instruction in Islamic sciences and Arabic language.
2. Raising the level of cultural and social life amongst the Muslims in Britain.
3. The establishment of a mosque so that Moslems can carry out their necessary duties and celebrate official religious holidays.
4. The founding of Muslims schools to teach the sons of Muslims the elements of Islam and reading and writing and the true Islamic culture.
5. The founding of an Arabic language reading room, and the provision of different kinds of Muslim publications.
6. The instruction of Muslim girls in schools especially made available to them, and the devotion of special care to them.
7. Raising the level of health and social reform amongst the Muslims in Britain.
8. Strengthening the cultural and social bonds between Muslims and non-Muslims.
9. Strengthening friendship and communications between

ASSALAM Vol. 1 No.28

ASSALAM A Weekly
Arabic Newspaper
Editor in Chief and
Director
Abdulla Ali El Hakimi

16 Peel Street, Cardiff
Tel. No. 1087
Address
Assalam Cardiff

Sunday 26 th. JUNE .19

صاحب الجريدة ومديرها
ورئيس تحريرها المؤلف
عبد الله علي الحكيمي ·
جميع المراسلات ترسل باسم
رئيس التحرير الى العنوان التالي

الاشتراكات
انظر ص ٥ ع ٤

جريدة عربية دينية ادبية ثقافية سياسية اخبارية

٢٦ يونيو ١٩٤٩   الاحد ٢٩ شعبان ١٣٦٨ ه   العدد ٢٨   السنة الاولى

كيف يجب ان يكونه الشباب الذى نتمناه الامة فى حالة نهضتها

حكمة الاسبوع

لا زوال للنعمة مع الشكر . ولا بقاءلها
مع الكفر

Muslims in Britain and those outside, and exchanging Islamic sciences and literature.

10. Sending groups of students to study in the Azhar University in Cairo, and in the Egyptian University so that they should complete their studies and return to their country to instruct other Muslims.

Most of these aims had indeed been achieved in the sixteen years from al-Hakimi's arrival in South Shields to his departure from Cardiff in 1952. There is a certain ambiguity in the concept of a 'Muslim School' since this could apply both to an actual building exclusively used for the purpose, and to a class held regularly in a private house. The former aim was not in the end realized, the latter and easier one was.

Al-Hakimi did not explicitly include in the aims of his Society the kind of nationalist political work in which he engaged in the late 1940s; but it was probably this kind of political activity that lay at the core of his plans when he left for the Middle East, even though he said in public that he was going to raise funds for his project. This political commitment must have been underlined by the fact that some time after he had decided to leave Cardiff the July 1952 nationalist military coup took place in Egypt. Al-Hakimi finally left Cardiff in August 1952 and visited Egypt later in the year: there he met with General Neguib the then leader of the military government, and Neguib is reported to have promised some financial aid for al-Hakimi's school. In December of that year his followers in Cardiff received a letter from him, containing this message: 'Stay united. Do not split from each other, or your good name and deeds will disappear.' He later left Egypt and went on to Aden where he met up with members of the Free Yemeni opposition who had fled from the North after 1948. On 2 April 1953 a public meeting was held in Aden to welcome him back. But things turned out badly in Aden: al-Hakimi was imprisoned for a time by the British authorities in 1953 on charges of having a revolver in his luggage – some said it had been planted by agents of the imam. Then, after his release and only two years after his departure from Cardiff, he died suddenly on 4 August 1954.[16]

Al Hakimi's achievement in organizing the Yemeni community in Britain was a striking one, above all because of the enterprise he showed in undertaking the various activities of his society, and it was one which found some echo in Yemen itself, since his newspaper was one of the few voices raised against the imam in the dark years between 1948 and the growth of the opposition in Aden in the mid 1950s. At least some copies of his paper were sent home. Al-Hakimi's ideas were those of a nationalist and reforming Islamic thinker, and are well illustrated in a speech he gave in Aden on his return. He reiterated themes familiar in the opposition of that time: the unnecessary decay of North Yemen, the failure of the imams to put through reforms, the dispersal of so many 'sons of Yemen' in search of work across the world. 'We are not against anyone,' he said, 'all we want is reform. . . . We would be prepared to support the Imam if he was ready to carry out reforms and to grant the requests of the Yemeni people.' He stressed the need for education and the terrible ignorance and fear that had befallen the people of Yemen, a land once known as 'Happy Yemen' (or *Arabia Felix*). 'Our people has been sleeping for a long time. It is paralysed: ignorance has followed knowledge and oppression has followed justice and poverty has followed wealth.' He also stressed the need for unity. Referring, by implication, to the effect of tribal and regional differences among Yemenis, he urged that there should be 'no Zeidis and no Shafeis, no Adnanis and no Qahtanis, no Somalis and no Adenis, no Jibalis and no Tihamis, no Lahejis and no Abyanis, no Beihanis and no Hadramis'.[17]

The language he used was that of classical Islamic thought. The greatest virtues were knowledge and justice, the greatest evils oppression [*dhulm*] and ignorance. Words like freedom and democracy, let alone socialism or imperialism, had not yet entered his political vocabulary in the way they were to do that of the Yemeni nationalist movement later in the decade. He spoke a clear, rather spare Arabic, free of the flat repetitions and rhetoric that characterized many of his successors. The path to his goals was through unity and reform, and he does not seem to have been particularly opposed even to monarchs: in the last issue of *al-Salam* he made a point of making a profession of his respect to Queen Elizabeth II, who had just succeeded to the throne, and his paper regularly carried accounts of the actions of kings in such Middle Eastern states as Jordan and Iraq. Although it was not men like al-Hakimi who were to lead the nationalist movements in North and South Yemen in the years that followed his death, he occupies a place of some importance in the period between the end of the Second World War and the mid 1950s, when Yemeni nationalism in South, North and among the exile communities was beginning to take shape.

The organization founded by al-Hakimi survived his departure. The continued vitality of the Allawi Society, which he founded, was evident when Dahya studied the Yemeni community in Birmingham in the early 1960s.[18] Dahya reports that a branch of the sect was set up in Birmingham in 1955–6 and had 250–300 members. Its statutes gave it three main functions: to provide aid to sick members to help them to return home; to buy property as trust investment for the Society; and to settle disputes among members according to Islamic law. It was this third function which in particular occupied the sheikh in authority in Birmingham, as he faced numerous cases of disputes within the migrant community: the disputants preferred the adjudication of an unofficial Islamic court to that of the official British courts. According to Dahya, the Birmingham branch of the Allawi Society had contact with those in other British cities, but acted as an autonomous body. Its greatest difficulty seemed to be that of containing the challenges to traditional authority that emerged from within the community from younger members; it was they who, it seems, were mainly responsible for setting up the secular nationalist organizations – of the kind studied in Chapter 4 – that began to emerge in the late 1950s and which were to consolidate themselves in the 1960s. In the 1940s it had been possible for al-Hakimi to combine religious organization and nationalist politics within the same framework, as it again became possible in the late 1970s and 1980s: in the late 1950s and early 1960s, however, the two forms of activism were less compatible.

In other respects, al-Hakimi's legacy in Britain was less durable. No one replaced him as an organizer until the emergence of quite different nationalist organizations among the workers in the 1960s and early 1970s. At the Nur al-Islam mosque no Sheikh came to take his place until 1965 when a new leader came from North Yemen: this sheikh, Abdul Kadir, was believed to have been appointed by al-Hakimi before the latter's death, but he did not stay long in Cardiff and the majority of the Arab community there had remained with Sheikh Hassan Ismail. The latter remained in Cardiff till 1956 and then left for North Yemen, where he died in 1959. His place, as spiritual leader of the main group of Yemenis, was taken by Sheikh Said, a young second-generation Muslim, of mixed Yemeni and British origin.

Cardiff in the 1970s

In the mid 1970s, thirty years after the foreign and Arab communities in the area reached their peak, little of old Butetown could be recognized. Homfray Street, just before the entrance to Butetown under the railway bridge, where Hajji Mahomet the Somali 'priest' hid on the roof during the 1919 riots, had been almost completely pulled down and was now shared between a parking lot and a garage. The railway bridge that marks the entrance to Butetown still stood, bearing on its southern face an appeal that was unlikely to attract the more devout Muslims that passed beneath: 'It's Brains You Want', it said, 'Brains Beer'. The Taff Vale Railway, which for a century brought coal to the prosperous docks, still rattled above Bute Street along which ran the orange buses of Cardiff Corporation, but most of the older buildings had vanished in the redevelopment. The only ones left were a few larger, derelict ones, just past the bridge, but beyond that there was a new council housing estate, with two fifteen-storey tower blocks on what was once Loudoun Square. There were none of the cafés that once made the area famous. In the 1940s K. S. Little discovered that different ethnic groups lived in distinct streets; but that no longer held. During the redevelopment Sheikh Said, leader of the majority group of Yemenis, tried to get special residential areas for the Muslims on the grounds that his followers could not tolerate either the cooking of bacon or people coming home drunk. But the council refused to allow this.

Al-Hakimi's Nur al-Islam mosque still stood but it was alone on a Peel Street that had otherwise disappeared. It bore an inscription in English and Arabic saying that the mosque was 'erected by the Islamia Allaouia Society, 1947 AD, 1355 AH'. Next to the mosque stood a betting shop and a public house. About a mile away, below Loudoun Square, stood a new *zawiya* erected in 1967. On it was a flag-pole with the green Islamic flag, and in Arabic a written sign: 'The Islamic Centre and Allawi Zawiya' [*al-Markaz al-Islamiya wa al-Zawiya al-Alawiya*].

The *zawiya* was the meeting place for many of those who formed the group around Sheikh Hassan Ismail in the conflict with al-Hakimi, and a certain distance persisted between the followers of the latter, who used the Nur al-Islam, and the followers of the former, who patronized the *zawiya*. But after thirty years the old issues had died down and, as one person rather gently put it, 'People are now beginning to get tired of the whole business.' In the *zawiya* building there was a reading-room where a half dozen or so Yemeni men read Islamic books and newspapers from Arab states; some who were retired spent all day there, in between prayers which were held in the mosque next door. The *zawiya* was run by Sheikh Said Hassan Ismail. Born in South Shields of an English mother and a Yemeni sailor father, who was drowned at sea during the Second World War, he moved to Cardiff as a child and was adopted by Sheikh Hassan Ismail. The latter trained him in Islamic thought and sent him for three years to Ta'iz in North Yemen. When Hassan Ismail left in 1956 Sheikh Said took over his responsibility; although his followers had for years to make do with a prayer-room in a private house, they were able in the late 1960s to get their *zawiya* built.

Sheikh Said, who himself worked as a welder in a Butetown factory, explained that in the *zawiya* 'we all feel that we are in Yemen'. The people who came to the *zawiya* were interested in two things: prayer and work, and he explained how nearly all Yemenis had stayed in the area during redevelopment because they wanted to be near the mosque. Most sent money home to their families, although in a country where modern banking had only begun to develop they did so in a peculiar way. They sent their money through a bank to an agent in Ta'iz, who took a 2 per cent commission on whatever he handled. He confirmed receipt of the money by letter, and was then held responsible for the delivery of the money to the various villages. If the money did not arrive, he had to pay up himself.

Sheikh Said recalled the development of nationalist consciousness among the community in Cardiff. The Suez events of 1956 had aroused considerable enthusiasm and many members of the community had sat up late at night listening to Cairo radio. Before that many Yemenis had had a defensive attitude to their background and some children had tried to conceal their background by saying they were 'Spanish'. After that, they were all proud to be 'Arabs', even though many of the younger ones could not speak more than a few words of Arabic. But 1956 also produced some hostility from British people working in factories with Arabs. They would say, 'Go back to b... Nasser'. The Yemenis would reply: 'If you don't watch out, he'll be here soon'. The workers in Cardiff collected money for the Egyptian cause, sending thousands of pounds to Cairo.

Sheikh Said also recalled the response to the 1962 events in North Yemen. He emphasized that, surprisingly in view of their attitude to al-Hakimi, the community had unanimously supported the overthrow of the imam and, like Yemeni exiles elsewhere, they had hoped that the new government would provide jobs and create the conditions for economic prosperity in the country. But the eight-year civil war dampened enthusiasm as did the continued economic stagnation of the country. People who went back reported that many things had not changed, although there had been a revival of hope after the military coup of June 1974, which had promised strong government. The new military ruler, Colonel al-Hamdi, was popular, but as one old man in the corner of the *zawiya* reading-room remarked: 'What Yemen needs is not one, but a hundred Hamdis.' Unfortunately for Yemen, al-Hamdi was not allowed to continue his reforming work and was assassinated in October 1977.

Although many of the members of the community had been living in Cardiff for decades, and only returned home on brief visits, the Yemenis kept in close touch through letters, newspapers and through listening to Ta'iz Radio. Talk was often of events at home, and as one younger member of the community remarked to me: 'They know more about what's happening in Ta'iz than on the other side of Cardiff.' At times this pride in Yemen took on a certain unreality: one old man began extolling the martial powers of the Yemenis and told me that if it had not been for obstruction by the King of Jordan, thousands of Yemenis would have invaded Israel during the 1967 Arab–Israeli war. Another issue that aroused spirits on a cold winter's evening in Butetown was the prospect of purchasing, on their return, the prize which is symbolic for many Yemeni men: a good gun. Indifferent to the fact that but a few weeks before the North Yemeni government had banned the carrying of firearms in Sana'a, two men began assuring me that as soon as they got home they would buy themselves a good machine gun. The current going price was, so they claimed, £300–350.

An illuminating picture of the Arab community came from Mrs Olive Suleiman, a Welsh woman who lived with her sons and grandchildren near Butetown. Her Yemeni husband had worked first as a camel tender in the British camel corps in Aden, had saved some money, and had then emigrated to France; after a year there, he had come on to Cardiff. He had never been a sailor, but was a cook, and he and Mrs Suleiman had run the Cairo Café in Butetown, a centre of Arab social life, for thirty-eight years. Mrs Suleiman herself had come from a village in the Welsh valleys and her mother had been warned by the local clergymen not 'to let her daughter marry a heathen'. However she did: she had twelve children, and now had a family of thirty-five. She had learnt to speak Arabic, had become a Muslim and after visiting her daughter who now lived in Ta'iz she made the pilgrimage or *hajj* to Mecca. She was never happier, she said, than when she could hear Arabic being spoken in the street, although she admitted she had never cared for Arabic food. She regretted that the old Butetown she had known had been killed by redevelopment.

One of the best-known members of the Yemeni community in Cardiff, and indeed in Britain, was Hajj Salih Hassan al-Udhaini, who lived in Loudoun Square. Born around 1908, he had come to Cardiff as a sailor in the 1920s and had later found work on a dredger in Cardiff docks. He was an expert in traditional Yemeni medicine which he practised according to special centuries-old books, using herbs and other substances sent specially from Yemen. Not only Yemenis, but also Pakistanis, Bengalis and Turks from London and the Midlands come to visit him and to have *djinns* exorcized. When I visited him, he was clad in his embroidered green Yemeni jacket and white robes and we were interrupted by a Pakistani family who had come to be treated by him. Hajj Salih had saved £350 to go to Mecca in 1966: there he had met King Feisal of Saudi Arabia, who had promised help to the effort of the Muslims in Cardiff. As was the practice, he had brought to Mecca the flag of the country he lived in, and he had therefore taken with him the Welsh flag. He believed that he was the first person ever to fly the Welsh flag at Mecca, and people had come to ask him what it was. 'They had only heard of London,' he said, ' and knew nothing of Cardiff. But I told them that I lived in the land of the Welsh and that this was the Welsh flag. The Welsh are a good people [*al-welsh nas tayyibin*]'. On his return a sheep had been killed in the street outside his house, and this had provoked the complaints of animal-loving members in the British community. The protagonist of this slaying was Hajj Salih's son Abdullah Mohammad, who was now living at home with his father.

Abdullah Mohammad had served for six years in the British Army and was a keen rugby player: 'I am the first Arab to play at Cardiff Arms Park,' he told me. His father had been to see him play once but had been upset because his son (who is a hooker) was always 'buried' by the others. As a young boy Abdullah Mohammad remembered the visit to Cardiff in October 1946 of the North Yemeni princes Saif al-Islam Abdullah and Seif al-Islam Yahya.[19] He himself had later been to North Yemen, in 1956, and had been shocked by the contrast between the Yemen he saw and the romantic picture projected by the older exiles in Cardiff. The poverty and corruption were especially striking, as was the somewhat desperate pursuit of alcohol: he had met men who drank mixtures of tomato juice and kerosene.

During his visit Abdullah Mohammad had travelled to visit the ferocious Imam Ahmad, in the company of a group of North Yemen students who had just come back from some time in Egypt. What happened sums up as well as anything the conflicts brewing in Yemen at that time. The students with whom Abdullah Mohammad was travelling were full of the new spirit of Arab nationalism and as they travelled to see the imam they were singing a popular song of the period, 'Freedom' ['*Horria*'], which had been made famous by the Egyptian singer Umm Kalthoum. They had decided that when they met the imam they would not kneel, as was traditional, but would greet him in the modern way by shaking his hand. When they entered the reception room, the first student went up to do just that. But the imam would have none of it. He sat on his throne, armed bodyguards at his side, and as the first student tried to shake hands the imam clouted him and jabbed his finger unambiguously at the floor. They all knelt down in turn: they were now at home. Abdullah Mohammad also met the imam's son, al-Badr, who, they said, appeared interested in reform, but was unable to do anything. On his return to Cardiff the disillusioned Abdullah tried to argue with the older members of the community and to contradict their account of North Yemen; but it took the 1962 republican coup to break through the exiles' illusions. Only then did Cardiff, in the land of the Welsh, catch up with Sana'a, in the real land of the Yemenis.

South Shields: The Mill Dam Riots and Beyond

Of equal importance to Cardiff in the history of Yemenis in Britain is the community in the port city of South Shields, at the mouth of the Tyne in north-east England. South Shields, and its twin across the river, North Shields, were close to the Tyneside centres of the shipbuilding industry and from the 1880s onwards it appears that an immigrant community of Chinese, Indians, Yemenis, Somalis and Africans had begun to settle there. The numbers rose during the First World War, but the postwar slump in demand for sailors led to clashes in South Shields, as it had in Cardiff. The issue was the familiar one of preference being given to white as against Arab seamen, and on 4 February 1919 violence broke out on the Mill Dam, the sea-front open space where sailors were hired. In the revealing words of the local paper:

> Turbulent scenes, the like of which have never before been seen in South Shields, were witnessed at the Mill Dam yesterday afternoon. The disturbances apparently originated amongst a number of Arab seamen who were seeking employment at the South Shields Shipping Office, and in an incredibly short space of time hundreds of people became involved in a fierce conflict which assumed alarming proportions, and necessitated the calling out of naval and military detachments.
>
> Numerous gangs of Arabs, armed with revolvers, knives and sticks and bottles, attacked the crowd, indiscriminately, and as far as can be ascertained, more than a dozen persons sustained injuries, though fortunately the revolver shots all went astray. ... The trouble seems to have arisen through a dispute which occurred during the signing on of a crew at the South Shields Shipping Office, when an Arab seaman, who had presented himself for engagement, was informed that only white men were required for the crew.[20]

THE SOUTH SHIELDS

NEW MOSQUE ISLAMIC TRUST FUND

The Trust Fund is under the control of an eleven-member Management Committee of an international nature, comprising:—
Three Pakistani, four Arab, three Somali, and (as Patron), His Worship The Mayor of South Shields.

Trustees:
S. G. H. SHAH (Pakistani), Chairman.
MOHAMED SAID (Arab), Treasurer.
IDE JAMMA (Somali), Joint Treasurer.
MOHAMED RAJHA (Arab), Secretary.
LUCKMAN ALI (Pakistani).

Solicitors:
Messrs. WINSKELL & WALKER,
King Street, South Shields.

Correspondence should be addressed to:—
S. G. H. SHAH, Chairman.
13 Renoir Gardens,
South Shields,
England.
Telephone: South Shields 3921

Donations to:—
NEW MOSQUE ISLAMIC TRUST FUND,
Lloyds Bank Ltd.
High Shields Branch,
Laygate,
South Shields,
England.

The Moslem Community in South Shields

Over fifty years ago Moslems from Arabia began to settle in the busy shipping port of South Shields, on the River Tyne, on the North East Coast of England. They were almost entirely employed on the many types of ships which use this port. After the First World War the community began to expand and was joined by Moslems from Somaliland, India, Egypt and Malaya.

Worship

Through the years, regular worship has continued, but has only been possible by using temporary rooms in various boarding houses and similar premises and constant moves from place to place have been necessary. It has never been possible to secure really suitable premises.

The Community expands

The size of the community has now risen to over seven hundred, increased at times to a thousand by the addition of visiting Moslem seamen.

The Third Generation . . . over 150 children

The Moslem leaders in South Shields, fully conscious of the need for a permanent place of worship, feel that even greater is the present need for a School, in which the children can be instructed in the Islamic Faith.

Building a New Mosque and School

As indicated on the previous page, a Fund to meet this need has now been set up . . . its aim, to raise not less than twenty thousand pounds, and, within five years, to have built an Eastern-style Mosque containing accommodation and providing facilities for both Worship and Teaching.

Will you help?

An appeal for help in this great work is made to all, far and near, who are interested in fostering and teaching the fundamentals of the Islamic Faith.

How you can help

Gifts, great and small, will be gratefully received and thankfully acknowledged.
Should you wish to have further information and, should you wish to hear of the progress of the scheme, the officers of the Trust Fund will be glad to hear from you and mail information to you.

Facing the future

Moslems, of all nations, all over the world, can help and the Management Committee of the Trust Fund firmly believe and trust that the necessary support will be forthcoming and they go forward with their plans, firm in the assurance that they will not trust in vain.

For and on behalf of
The South Shields Moslem Community,
Yours very truly,
SAYYAD GHULAM HASSON SHAH
Chairman of the Committee.

Appeal for the South Shields New Mosque Islamic Trust Fund.

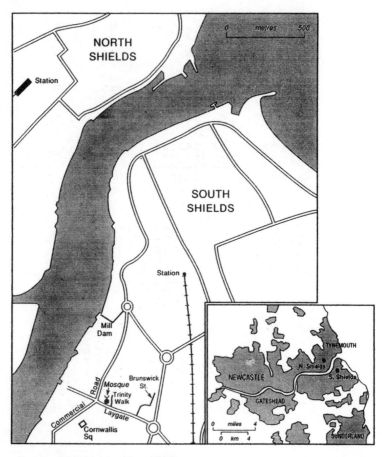

South Shields in the 1980s.

As a result of this incident, thirteen Arabs were charged with riot. The names of those accused left little doubt as to where they were from – they were Yemenis: Muhammad Ali, fireman; Muhammad Salih, fireman; Abdul Said, fireman; Muhammad Hassan, donkeyman were among the sailors charged, as were two boarding-house keepers, Ahmad Ali and Ali Hassan.

If the conflicts of 1919 were part of a broader pattern of conflict in British ports after the First World War, the second major incident in South Shields had a more specific character. This was a dispute of an even more markedly political nature which broke out in 1930 as a result of the introduction by the National Union of Seamen of a rota for non-white sailors, designed to exclude those who could not prove British nationality.[21] In this conflict, the Yemenis were supported by the Seamen's Minority Movement (a group supported by the Communist Party and others) which was trying to organize a boycott of the shipping offices until the rota system was abandoned. Matters came to a head in early August 1930. After two weeks of peaceful picketing of the shipping office on the Mill Dam by Yemeni and British supporters of the Movement, a major clash broke out on 2 August, when the protesting crowd of around 150 Yemenis and 100 whites tried to stop two white seamen from signing on. A boarding-house owner, Ali Said, was acting as leader and translator for the Yemenis. At one point, R. O'Donnell, a Minority Movement Leader, turned to the crowd and shouted that he was ashamed of being British because 'the Arabs are standing out 100 percent and the white men are still signing on.' Clashes between the pickets and police followed; Yemenis were arrested at the scene, and some white organizers and sailors later. In all, twenty-seven men – twenty-one Yemenis and six whites – were later charged on a variety of offences: incitement to riot, riot and obstructing the police. In subsequent trials, a number of Yemenis were sentenced to hard labour and later deportation.

These demonstrations produced considerable discussion in the local press, and voices hostile and favourable to the Yemeni sailors were heard. One correspondent wrote attacking the boarding-house keepers as 'crimps', i.e. people who forced men onto ships, and asserted: 'we intend to eliminate them . . . purely and simply'. Others charged that the Arabs could not work, and that they produced knives 'on the slightest provocation'. Thus 'Fair Play' wrote: 'I say Britishers can work better than an Arab anytime, and it is about time they were all sent back where they came from'. Voices with another message were, if anything, more common. Thus a B. Williams from London wrote:

These Arabs are part and parcel of our Empire, and it is the duty of every Britisher worth his salt to see to it that they get a sporting chance . . . the non-registration of these men for employment is absurd, and reflects ill upon our hospitality. We allow foreigners from every land to work here in Britain, and it seems that some people would prefer a Russian or other nondescript to an Arab, whose forefathers brought civilisation to Darkest Europe.

The wife of an Arab sailor wrote in reply to 'Fair Play': 'Half the Englishmen on the dole are there through their own fault, being too lazy to look for work. . . They are forgetting it is the coloured man's country they depend on. What would England do if Arabs were to do the same to them as England is doing to the Arabs?'. Others stressed the social responsibility of the Arab community. 'I have never seen one Arab yet who has left his wife and family hungry to enjoy a good night in a public house. An Arab thinks too much of his religion to make a mockery of himself'. And a correspondent with the name 'Sea Dog' intervened: 'As master and mate of ships for forty years I can honestly say I never saw an Arab the worse for drink on board'.[22]

Following this incident, there was further public controversy in South Shields, this time over the eligibility of Yemeni sailors for poor house relief. In the normal course of events, Yemenis who could not find employment on ships would be supported by their boarding-house owners, but the impact of the depression and of the new rota system brought special hardship in 1930. In late September 1930, ninety-seven Yemenis entered the Harton Institution, the local poor house, amid much protest from the local press and rate payers. The reply of the poor house authorities was revealing: it reported that the number of Arabs, Somalis and Indians currently in South Shields now stood at 563, compared to an earlier figure of 2000; of these 90 were permanent residents, and 470 were seamen who had now registered on the rota. While some of those who wrote to *The Shields Daily Gazette and Shipping Telegraph* were critical of the decision to help the Yemeni sailors, two contrary voices were heard.[23] One was from Said Mabrouk, a boarding-house keeper of 2 Laygate Street, South Shields, who wrote to say:

I very much regret that certain town's people are blaming all the Arab boarding house keepers for getting the best out of the Arab seamen and now shifting their burden on to the ratepayers. This, of course, is not true, as I, for one, have kept an Arab boarding house for the past ten years and have always kept my men together, and I am still doing so. Not one of my 44 boarders has applied for relief. I have kept them through many difficulties and I still intend to do so. There is also a statement that a number of Arabs and their white wives and families are living in the Arab boarding houses. As far as my house is concerned I have no married Arabs and families in my house, and I do not know of any other boarding house that has them. I think the person who is responsible for this statement has been misinformed and does not know much about the Arab community.

The other voice was that of O'Donnell, an organizer of the Minority Movement and one of those charged after the 2 August riot. He wrote to say that the responsibility for the Arabs needing to apply for relief lay with the National Union of Seamen and the imposition of the rota system, and continued:

There has been talk of sending them back to their own country. But why are they here? Why is it that in their country, as stated by 'Mariner', they go about in loin cloths and eat mealies? They were brought here for exploitation to earn fat profits for the shipowners. But owing to having to exploit them in this country they could not, for fear of public opinion, exploit them to the extent of their only being able to afford loin cloths and mealies.

The Second World War brought new demand for Yemeni sailors in the Merchant Navy but, in contrast to Liverpool, it does not seem to have led to any further settlement in South Shields. Collins, who studied the community in the 1950s, reported even then that there had been no new settlement for some decades, and this remained true thereafter.[24] What did persist was a community of some hundreds of Yemenis, organized around their boarding houses and religious activities, and who, like those in Cardiff, intermarried with British women and produced a second and third generation. In 1943 the community acquired a mosque, in a converted pub, on Cuthbert Street, which until its demolition in 1961 served as the centre for the Allawi Society's activities promoted by al-Hakimi. A new, temporary, mosque was opened on Brunswick Street, and it was reported that at its opening four leaders of the Yemeni religious community were present: Sheikh Abdul Ali, the imam of South Shields, Sheikh Said Hassan Ismail from Cardiff, Sheikh Muhammad Qasim from Birmingham and an unnamed imam from Hull. This probably gives a good idea of the leadership of the Allawi Society in the early 1960s. The South Shields community hoped to move quickly to a new mosque on a site set aside for this purpose in Laygate Street, but difficulties and disputes within the mosque committee delayed the opening of this new building until 1972. Conflict over the building of the mosque seems to have involved both disputes within the Yemeni community (between more traditional and more politically active members) and a growing division within the Muslim community as a whole between the Yemenis and Somalis on one side, and the increasingly dominant Pakistani community on the other.

Liverpool: On 'The Street of the Yemenis'

Liverpool was at one time the busiest port in the British Empire and was from the 1900s onwards host to a small but distinctive Yemeni community. Like Cardiff it owed its prosperity to the docks, and it was this which attracted immigrants from all over the British Isles and Empire. Liverpool's original prosperity in the eighteenth century was based on the slave trade; but despite the decline in slaving in the early nineteenth century, it continued to grow. It was the outlet for the goods of industrial Lancashire, and until the growth of Southampton at the end of the century it was the main transatlantic departure point from Britain and much of northern Europe. The port began to decline after the First World War, and because of the absence of much local industry it provided relatively little employment for the new immigrants who came to Britain after the Second. In Liverpool, as in Cardiff and South Shields, communities made up of ageing sailors still survive, but in contrast to the two larger but declining communities, Liverpool's immigrant population expanded in the postwar period as a result of an influx from Yemeni communities elsewhere in Britain.

The Yemenis in Liverpool were part of a much broader immigration process. Figures compiled after the First World War

Table 4 Non-English Population of Liverpool 1921

	%
Ireland	33.0
Wales	27.4
Scotland	17.0
Isle of Man/Channel Islands	6.0
Dominions and Colonies	5.4
Foreign Countries	11.3

Source: The Social Survey of Merseyside, ed. D. Caradog Jones, Liverpool 1934, p. 77.

show that about 10 per cent of the population had come from outside England, but that the majority of this 10 per cent came from other parts of the British Isles (Table 4).

The Arabs living in Liverpool, or based there between periods at sea, were found both among the citizens of the British Empire – the 5.4 per cent from the Dominions and Colonies – and among the citizens of foreign countries, but there are only fragmentary details of both. Most of those from the Empire, totalling around 6000, were Canadians, Australians and West Africans, but there were also some 'lascars', among whom must have been the Yemenis and Somalis. Because they were a small part of the colonial population they were never registered separately. There are, however, figures on other Arabs who were classified as aliens, although again they formed a small minority, compared to the largest foreign communities – the Russians (2900 in 1921), citizens of the USA (1500) and the Poles (1100). A combination of police returns and census data give the figures shown below (Table 5) for Egyptians and Turks over fifty years of Liverpool's greatest prosperity, and one can assume that since 'Turk' referred to any citizen of the Ottoman Empire, this must until the First World War have included people from such countries as Syria, Lebanon, Iraq and Palestine. Further figures of a rough kind are also available from the police returns. For 1930 and 1938 respectively there were eight-three and eighty-six people registered as falling into a generic Middle East group which covered virtually all the countries of the area: 'Egyptians, Armenians, Liberians, Iraquians, Palestinians, Turks, Ottomans, Iranians, Persians, Syrians'.[25] It is obvious from this list, of course, that the enumerators were all too hazy about where these people came from. Liberians are not from

Table 5   Egyptians and Turkish Citizens in Liverpool, 1881–1930

	Egyptians	Turks	Area Covered
1881	8	44	Liverpool & Birkenhead
1891	23	62	Liverpool & Birkenhead
1901	9	48	Merseyside
1911	110	239	Merseyside
1921	107	17	Merseyside
1930	56	29	Police Returns

the Middle East, while Turks are the same as Ottomans, and Persians are Iranians.

The Arab communities in Liverpool lived in those areas where the other non-white sailors and their families settled and, as in Cardiff, tended to be separated off from the rest of the population. The largest non-white communities were the Chinese, who came before the First World War, the West Africans and the West Indians. By 1954 there were reckoned to be under 1000 members of the Chinese community and about 6000 other non-white immigrants and their descendants. However, although there has been quite a lot of research on race relations and immigration in Liverpool, very little attention has been devoted to the Arab immigrants; one reason is that they formed a less substantial grouping, in both absolute and relative terms, than they did in their two main centres, Cardiff and South Shields.

There seem to have been three waves of Yemeni immigration into Liverpool, two associated with the booms in the shipping trade, and the third, much more recent, with openings in the service-sector trade. The first wave was up to and including the First World War, after which Liverpool experienced decline and, in 1919, anti-alien riots. This first influx of Arabs – from Egypt and Lebanon, as well as from Yemen and Somalia – was smaller and resulted in a less coherent settled community than in Butetown. During the Second World War there was another increase in the demand for Yemenis to serve in British ships and again a considerable, but temporary, increase in the numbers of Arabs in Liverpool occurred. In the 1970s there was a small Yemeni and Somali community of ageing sailors, but because Liverpool, unlike Cardiff, was still an international port, sailors from other Arab countries, especially Egypt, visited on a short-term basis. The largest Yemeni grouping was, however, a third and quite distinct one, a new generation of Yemeni shopkeepers and service-sector workers who had come to Liverpool within the past decade.

In the mid 1970s most of these Arabs lived in or around the district known as Liverpool 8, where the majority of the overseas non-white immigrants had settled; and although not physically sealed off in the way Butetown was, Liverpool 8 was socially sealed off in much the same way. The difference was that Liverpool 8 had not yet been fully redeveloped, and it was in a rundown backstreet that had been built some time in the reign of Queen Victoria that I came across a seamen's lodging house of a kind that has disappeared elsewhere, except in South Shields. In the back room of this terraced house five old men sat around a coal fire – even though it was in the middle of May. Three were from North Yemen, one from Somalia and one from India. They were living on their pensions, and were not going back to their countries because, it seems, they had lost contact with their families there. The kitchen was old and it seemed nothing had changed there for thirty years or more. On the wall was a colour postcard of the town of Ibb, in the 'middle region', and on the wall-cupboard someone had scribbed 'Allah'. The former owner of the house was present: he no longer cooked for the people there, even though, as he pointed out, it was a point of honour among the sailors before that they did not cook for themselves.

The old sailors there had worked on the coal-burning ships in crews of sixteen and had got their jobs through an agent called Hamid Mohammed who had been based in Steamer Point, Aden. The Somali sailors had come from the British part of Somalia to Aden and had then signed on a ship. One Somali complained that he used to go to the Somali Club and Restaurant nearby, but now felt it had been taken over by English hippies. The sailors also remembered a Yemeni ship-owner, Ahmad al Hubadhi, from Rada in North Yemen, who had been based in Liverpool after the war: he had hired Yemenis on his ships and had contributed to al-Hakimi's fund-raising as well as to that of the Yemeni Prince Seif al-Islam Abdullah, when the latter visited Liverpool in 1946. As we were talking of the war period, one old sailor remarked that the names of all those drowned at sea during the Second World

War were inscribed on a monument down on the seafront. When we got down there he could not at first find it – the area had been rebuilt since his last visit years ago – but we finally came across it. On the monument were thousands of names – English, Irish, Chinese, Malay, and scores of Arab names, probably over a hundred. Ahmad Ismail had gone down in HMS *Highflyer*. Sheikh Yusuf Mohammad and Ali Mohammed Saleh had died in HMS *Jufair*. A whole crew of seventeen Yemenis had gone down in HMS *Fiona*, as they had in the Merchant Navy ship *Chakdina* and in others. It was a strange sight as the old man moved sadly and slowly over the dark monument, picking out the names of sailors he had known, the sons of Ibb and Rada and Dhala, whose bones now lay somewhere beneath the icy waters of the Atlantic.

Even in the 1970s there were only a handful of Yemeni and Somali sailors left in Liverpool; far more numerous was the new generation of shopkeepers who had come in the 1960s and early 1970s. By 1976 there were at least 100 of these – most in Liverpool 8, but some in Huyton, Bootle, Garston and other areas surrounding Liverpool. Granby Street in Liverpool 8 had no less than twelve shops run by Arabs. As one local shopkeeper remarked to me: 'In Amman, the capital of Jordan, they have their Street of Yemenis [*Sharih al-Yamaniyin*]. Here we have one too, and this is it.' A breakdown of these shopkeepers in the street revealed the pattern behind their settlement. The eleven Yemenis had all come between 1964 and 1973, though they had emigrated to Britain in the 1950s: they had worked for some years in factories, and had then come to Liverpool and bought shops, usually from English owners. The period before coming to Liverpool was spent not saving money, but acquiring contacts and knowledge in England. The money to set up the business was acquired on loan from other Yemenis or from a local branch of one of the British banks, which had special relations with the Liverpool Yemeni community. Seven out of the twelve shops were general stores, two were newsagents, and there was one butcher, one greengrocer and one wholesaler. Of the eleven Yemenis, four were from Dhala in the South, and four from the Nawa/Juhn region of North Yemen. The one exception in origin and time of arrival was a Sudanese who had arrived in 1950; he had previously been a sailor not a factory worker, and represented a tenuous connection with the previous generation of Arab immigrants. But the majority of this new generation of shop-keepers had worked in Birmingham and Sheffield in the 1950s and had then moved on to shopkeeping.

The interesting question about this community is why it was possible for a group of Yemeni shopkeepers to develop in Liverpool. Yemeni shopkeepers could be found elsewhere – in Birmingham, Sheffield, South Shields – but in these cities they served the Yemeni communities. Although there was some Arab connection with Liverpool already, this does not seem to have been the reason for this group settling there, since the majority of the Yemeni shopkeepers' customers were British people or members of other immigrant groups in Liverpool 8 and the surrounding areas. Moverover, even where such Yemeni shops did appear, the existence of Yemeni communities in other towns had not in the main led to the emergence of a large Arab shopkeeping class: there the shopkeepers were mainly British or South Asian. The most likely explanation is that precisely because Liverpool was not an area of large-scale immigration from South Asia and the West Indies the Yemenis were able to find an opening which was less available in other towns; and once one or two Yemenis got established they helped others from elsewhere in Britain or coming directly from their village and area to follow. This pattern continued throughout the 1970s and 1980s. Although Liverpool 8 – and Granby Street, in particular – were the scene of major rioting in July 1981, the Yemeni shops were largely left alone. And in the ensuing years dozens more Yemenis set up shops in the area.

By the early 1990s, the Liverpool grouping had become one of the largest Yemeni communities in Britain: in contrast to the other main centres, whether maritime or industrial, where population stagnated or fell in the 1980s, the Liverpool community grew to reach around 3500 in 1992. Yemenis who had lost employment elsewhere came to run shops in the Liverpool area, and there were now reckoned to be at least 130 of these: but the community also expanded with the arrival of family members from Yemen, as state and social controls on emigration eased, and with the arrival of the second and third generations born in Britain. Certain features of the early 1970s community had changed: there were fewer shopkeepers, only four now on Granby Street itself, and the Yemeni club, the *al-Ahram*, had been closed after a fire. Yet some of the institutions of the community had also been consolidated: there had earlier been a *zawiya* at St. James' St., and between 1958 and 1972 a mosque, the Masjid al-Rahma, was constructed, in part with Yemeni financial support. It now had a Jordanian sheikh and a mixed, Yemeni and Pakistani, congregation. There was a Yemeni school, funded by the council, which taught some of the Yemeni women English in a hired hall and a core of people, including retired shopkeepers and one or two Yemeni doctors who had settled in the city, were planning to set up a community association. These Liverpool Yemenis were aware that other immigrants in the city – Chinese, Irish, West Indians – had been able to get council support, and they knew too that the Sheffield Yemeni community had been successful in this respect. Since 1978, Ethiopian *qat* was regularly available, and distributed by a Yemeni supplier. But there were also new issues of concern. These included the fact that many of the younger members of the community knew little or no Arabic: the diversion of scarce income and time, here as elsewhere, into the chewing of *qat*; the division between the mainstream of the community and a newer grouping derived from *al-Islah* (Reform), a party in Yemen itself which received support from Saudi Arabia and was propagating an Islamist politics; the problems created by the fact that British pensions paid to people now living in Yemen and sent through the banks were exchanged at the official rate of 18 rials to the pound, as against 55 rials on the free market. But what was perhaps most striking in talking to members of the community was the sense that despite the passage of time and the changes in the community itself, the link with Yemen, now a united country, was for many as strong as ever. Its problems were theirs and with the coming of some oil money and the promise of democratic elections, its prospects were theirs too. News of developments in the homeland was eagerly followed, and discussed.

The characteristics found in these three communities of Yemenis apply to the other ports where Arabs settled. There much smaller communities existed: in Hull, where there was still in the mid 1970s a Yemeni sheikh and about 50 Yemeni residents;[26] in Glasgow, where in the early 1950s there was a Yemeni restaurant at 23 Cranston Street, run by a Mohammad Thabet bin Thabet; in Southampton; and in Aldgate East, London, where a group of fifty or so Yemenis gathered around The Welcome Café until the early

1980s (see Chapter 5). However, after 1945 these sailor communities were the products of a previous age – of the high tide of British maritime power which bore these Yemeni and Somali sailors to the ports of England, Scotland and Wales. After 1945 that tide had receded, leaving these communities reduced and stranded. The subsequent history of the Yemeni communities in Britain lay elsewhere, in the industrial towns which attracted thousands of new immigrants from the Yemens in the two decades after the Second World War.

Chapter 3

Yemenis in Industrial Cities: The Pattern of the 1970s

An Immigrant Minority

As we have seen in Chapter 1, between one and two million immigrants mainly from Asia and the Caribbean came to Britain after the Second World War, and the second wave of Yemeni emigration to Britain was part of this larger influx. The largest components of the postwar immigration were from Asian societies that bear some similarities to North and South Yemen – from India, Pakistan, Bangladesh. But there were also substantial numbers of immigrants from the Caribbean, Cyprus, Malta, Poland, Italy and, continuously, from Ireland. Overall a great uprooting of peasants from less developed countries took place; in contrast to the myths of many in the importing countries this was a process carried out above all in response to the *demand* of these countries. Behind this movement of labour, into both Britain and the countries of Western Europe, lay above all the demand for workers to undertake the less rewarding tasks of an advanced industrial society: dirty, sometimes dangerous, lower-paid jobs which the indigenous working classes have become increasingly reluctant to take on. In this way, in two decades, a new lower stratum of the working class was created – one that was set apart by its position in the process of production and its predominantly unskilled character, by its immigrant origin and, often, by different coloured skin.

The second wave of Yemeni immigration to Britain was both typical and untypical of the postwar immigrant community as a whole. Like the Pakistanis and Bengalis, they came from peasant backgrounds and gravitated to unskilled employment in factories, and to residence in the more depressed areas of cities – nineteenth-century districts that had housed three or four generations of British people before them. Like most other immigrants, they came from British colonies. But here the resemblances end.

First of all, the Yemenis were a much smaller community than the others: at most they were 15,000 in number, a tenth the size of the Cypriot community, and only 2 per cent of the West Indians or South Asians.[1] From this two consequences follow. First, they remained rather invisible, not only to the indigenous British population but to other immigrants as well. Classified with Indians as 'lascars' before the First World War, they now became part of a generic 'black' or 'Asian' mass. Yemenis themselves report that they are sometimes called 'Pakky' by British workers; on one occasion, in a Pakistani kebab shop in Birmingham, the man behind the counter automatically began talking Urdu to my Yemeni companion.

A second consequence is that the occupational spread of the Yemenis was rather narrow. Most immigrant groups tended to gravitate towards one or other branch of employment but they were nevertheless distributed quite broadly through different branches of both services and industry. This was true of the Irish, Pakistanis, West Indians and Indians. Yemenis, by contrast, were almost wholly confined to unskilled or semi-skilled labour in engineering factories. There are of course several different categories of engineering work, but it is still striking that engineering is only one of several industrial areas in which non-white workers have played a major role. This occupational concentration ties into another specific feature of the Yemeni community: whereas over half of all postwar non-white immigrants settled in London and the South-East, virtually no Yemenis did. There was a small Yemeni community in Aldgate East in London, but this was only a few dozen strong and was a relic of an earlier, sailor, grouping. The postwar Yemeni immigrants went to industrial towns where there was engineering work: to Birmingham, Sheffield, Manchester in the main, and in small numbers to Coventry, Middlesborough and Scunthorpe. Here they formed part of much larger immigrant communities. But as part of this occupational focus, there were no Yemenis in other comparable towns of immigrant settlements – in Leicester,

Nottingham and Bradford for example, or in London and its environs.

The most important aspect of the Yemeni community, one which is discussed at greater length in Chapter 6 and which separated them off from most other immigrants for a very long time, is that they were 'sojourners': they did not consider they had come to Britain to settle. Although they might spend thirty years of their adult life here, they came to make money, save as much as possible, send it home, and then with luck, leave again. They had much tighter links with their home country than most other immigrants, and for this and other reasons had fewer links with the broader society in Britain of which they were a part.[2] The conventional pattern was for a Yemeni to come to Britain for a period of three to five years, and then to go home for a long stay of eight months or a year, before coming back to Britain again. Very few brought their families to Britain, and virtually all intended to go home when they retired. Perhaps the nearest comparable grouping were the Pakistanis: they too sent money home and maintained close ties with their families and villages. But whether they went home on visits or not many also tried to bring their families to Britain and to settle here. This was therefore a significant difference between them and the Yemenis; only in the late 1970s and 1980s did this particularism begin to change, and some Yemenis begin to conform to the pattern of other immigrants.

Whether or not, left to themselves, the Yemenis would have stayed, the pattern of their emigration was affected by the changing regime determining residence in Britain. Up to 1962 they could come and go as they pleased, and, had immigration remained uncontrolled, there would probably have been a larger turnover within the Yemeni community. The imposition of immigration controls by the British government in that year interrupted the natural coming and going of the Yemenis, and those that were already working in Britain found themselves stranded here. Since no others could take their place, they were forced to choose between losing income from Britain or staying themselves for the rest of their lives. Economic conditions in their homeland decided the question for most of them, and they stayed. They formed a community of men who had come before 1962, those who got through the gap before it was closed.[3]

The Postwar Influx

There exists a tenuous connection between the Yemeni communities of the postwar period and the earlier, sailor, ones. At the end of the Second World War and in the years immediately after, the demand for Yemeni sailors declined – as it had done after 1918. Once they got tired of waiting for more employment on ships, some sailors moved into industrial employment in the larger towns of the Midlands and North, since it was in these areas that employment opportunities were opening up. In the Balsall Heath area of Birmingham I met a man in 1975 who exemplified this pattern and claimed to be the oldest Yemeni inhabitant of the city. Qasim Abdul, from Makbana in the 'middle region', had first come to Britain as a sailor in 1925. He had served in the Merchant Navy till he was wounded and shipwrecked off the coast of Japan during the Second World War. On his return to his home port, Hull, he found it impossible to find work and in this way he came to Birmingham, with his Yorkshire-born wife, in 1944. There he got a job in a metal-working factory. Because he was invalided out of the merchant navy he was two or three years in advance of other Yemeni sailors; but even if he were not the first, he indicated the period and manner in which a few of the sailors moved into industrial employment and forged a link between the two waves of Yemeni emigration.

This link was not, however, the main reason for the influx of Yemenis into industrial employment in the postwar period. The major factors at work seem to have been the *general* increase in demand by factories which accounts for the flow of so many immigrants, and the special 'push' factors in North and South Yemen discussed in Chapter 1, the 1948 revolt and the boom in Aden. When exactly they came is not clear, but it seems that most came in the 1950s and in the years up to 1962. Dahya writes that in the early 1950s there were sixty to sixty-five Yemenis in Birmingham, living in six to seven houses in Balsall Heath, and that by the early 1960s there were around 1200 Northerners and 900 Southerners in the city. One man who came from Dhala told me he had come to Birmingham in 1954 and there were then only twenty or so Yemenis from both North and South in the city; on the other hand, very few indeed had come after 1962. It is important to remember in considering the immigration ban of

1962 that this, like the earlier demand, had in the eyes of the Yemenis themselves a Yemeni as well as a British component. 1962 was the year in which the imamate was finally overthrown in North Yemen, and when the opposition trade union movement in Aden acquired a powerful ally across the border, in the republican North. The threat to the British positions in Aden was therefore strengthened, and the nationalist movement among Yemenis consequently grew. Whether or not the 1962 revolution would in any case have contributed to lessening immigration of Yemenis into Britain, the fact that the two events came together led many Yemenis to see the 1962 ban as specifically directed against them.

All of these migrants were, so far as is known, peasants – men who had spent their childhood in the villages of the mountains north of Aden and who had herded goats and sheep for their fathers. According to Dahya, they were almost all tribal commoners, with a few from the religious nobility or *seyyids*. They tended to be second or third sons, the eldest remaining to inherit. The majority come from the 'middle region' of North Yemen or adjoining areas in the South, to the north of Aden: one estimate of the Birmingham community in the mid 1960s was that 800 had come from the North and 400 from the South.[4] Most came to England by arrangement with a relative or fellow villager already here and most financed the trip by borrowing from their families or friends. In the early 1950s they tended to come by sea – not working their passage as the earlier sailors had done, but as steerage passengers. Later they came on chartered planes; when they arrived they were met by a relative or acquaintance who gave them somewhere to live and helped them find a job in a factory. This pattern, 'chain migration', helps to explain the fact that men from one village would live in a house together and that in a factory there would also be a high incidence of men coming from the same village or two.

Industrial Employment

The kinds of jobs to which Yemenis went and in which they remained were characteristic of immigrant employment patterns in both postwar Britain and Europe. Although, as already indicated, the employment of Yemenis has been more restricted than that of other groups, it follows a certain general pattern, five aspects of which can be mentioned here.

1. Yemenis were found in unskilled and semi-skilled jobs of the kind progressively abandoned by British workers in the previous two decades, and in which immigrants are generally found. Figures for the West Midlands (an area that includes Birmingham) for 1966 show that 55 per cent of Pakistani workers were in unskilled manual employment, and another 24.4 per cent in semi-skilled manual jobs.[5] Figures for Algerian workers in France in 1968 show a similar distribution in that 54 per cent were unskilled labourers and a further 33.6 per cent semi-skilled.[6] Yemenis tended to approximate most closely to the Pakistanis and Bengalis in that they were more concentrated in these branches than the Indians or West Indians who had a higher percentage of skilled workers among them. Once in such employment, very few Yemenis were able to move up the employment scale. Of the 2000 or so first-generation Yemenis in Birmingham in the mid 1970s it appears that only one became a white-collar worker. In line with the experience of other groups and of Arabs in France, the Yemenis discovered that even if some could become skilled workers none would become foremen or supervisors. There was a general resistance by British employers to having immigrant workers as foremen because of hostility from British unions. In the case of Yemenis this was made more difficult by the fact that in most factories they formed a minority of the work-force; these factories would therefore not have a Yemeni supervisor, even on the grounds that one would be useful to 'control' the Yemeni workers.

2. Yemenis, like other needy immigrant workers, often preferred to work night-shifts and to do so on a permanent basis. Wages were higher – time and a third – and it was a form of work which men who were married tend to prefer not to work. But whereas among many factory work-forces there was a system of alternating night- and day-shifts, a permanent night-shift operated among Yemenis, and among many Pakistanis too, as the following observation on Pakistani textile workers in Bradford bears out:

It is interesting that permanent night work should predominate over the system of alternative days and night shifts as a working arrangement. This appears to be directly related to the availability of a migrant labour supply since the social and familial demands on them were at a minimum when they first arrived and were willing because the extrinsic reward was slightly higher to undertake work on this basis as a temporary measure. Once organized in this work, even with the changes in the social circumstances of the migrants, this arrangement developed into a permanent feature and so lessened the problems of employers using this system.[7]

For many Yemenis, therefore, the day began sometime between four in the afternoon and seven in the evening, when they rose, prepared their sandwiches to take to the factory, and left for work. When most of the city in which they lived was waking and going to work, the Yemenis were returning home to sleep.

3. Most Yemenis were employed on a personal basis, through someone they knew in the factory, who introduced them to the management. There were several reasons why this system operated for Yemenis, as it did for other immigrants coming to Britain. A Yemeni newly arrived in Britain could speak no English, let alone read or write it. He was therefore extremely unlikely to be able to negotiate his way through a Labour Exchange. In addition, a considerable number of firms maintained colour bars in their employment policy, so that whatever his qualification a non-white worker would not be employed. Knowing this, workers would be reluctant to apply to a firm where they knew no one, either via the Exchange or by presenting themselves at the factory gate. Added to these factors was the natural desire of a worker in an alien world to choose to work among fellow countrymen, if that were possible. The 1950s were a period of full employment and factories were then quite willing to recruit in this way, on the basis of workers whose judgement they trusted. An informal guarantee also existed in that a worker who did recommend a friend to a factory would have an incentive to make sure that those he recommended worked hard; if they did not, the management would be less likely to accept his recommendations in the future.

4. Yemenis who worked in British factories for years still had very little contact with many aspects of British society. In

particular, they had normally acquired a very sparse understanding of the English language. Surprising as this may be at first sight, it can be explained by a simple factor: the immigrant could fulfil his goals without doing so and had, therefore, no reason to learn English. He did not need it to find and keep a job or a house, or to shop. In the few situations where English might be essential, in filling out documents or in dealing with law courts or the police, community interpreters could be used. There was, moreover, a circular process at work. Because the worker did not know English, he naturally chose to live and work in situations where English was not needed. Once housed and employed within a 'Yemeni' context, he had no reason to use English, and little occasion for doing so. Here there is a contrast with even the earlier sailor communities who did learn English on the ships where they worked and from the English-speaking women with whom most of them lived. The Yemeni industrial worker lived in a more enclosed community.

In the workplace, Yemenis did learn to use a vocabulary of a very limited kind. Phrases like 'No Vacancies', 'shut up', 'no messing about', and words such as 'gaffer',[8] a 'union', 'shop steward', as well as terms of abuse were understood by virtually all workers. But most of the tasks they performed as unskilled workers could be shown to them either by fellow Yemenis or by sign-language, and the example of others could make up for a lot. If something new had to be said, it required only one Yemeni who did know a bit of English to translate to the others. Probably the first Yemenis who came to a factory did have to learn some English; they therefore provided a kind of shield for the others.

It is unclear, however, how far a process of linguistic blockage really occurred: while Yemenis rarely spoke English, and even more rarely wrote it, this did not mean that the passive understanding of it was also undeveloped. All Yemenis spent hours every week watching television – it was permanently on in the living-rooms of their homes – and they may have acquired a considerable passive understanding in this way. In any case, their Arabic was eroded by the gradual inclusions of English words or Arabicized versions of these. In addition to the phrases and words mentioned already, there were words such as 'tax' and 'bus' which are used in spoken Arabic, as well as words that were slightly altered to confirm to Arabic usage – *bolis* and *bark* [*police* and *park* (a car), there being no 'p' in Arabic], and *karasa* [to *cross* a road, here used in an Arabic verb form]. Native Yemenis who had not lived abroad tended to complain about the mongrel speech of their compatriots who returned from England, but English people will be struck by a curious if inverted parallel, that of English colonials who lived for years in India and the Arab world and who, although unable to speak Hindu or Arabic properly, would litter their spoken language with words and phrases borrowed from the speech of the people among whom they were living. Whatever the differences in social situation, in linguistic practice, an analogous process seems to have operated.

5. Much of the discussion of 'coloured' or 'black' workers in Britain has focused on the manner in which they are confined to the unskilled and semi-skilled occupations by a variety of discriminations.[9] From the point of view of identifying inequalities in the country of immigration this is a correct emphasis, but in so doing it obscures a further question within which there is also prejudice and incomprehension. These migrants worked in British factories of a modern industrial kind; as many studies have shown, they worked extremely hard and for long hours, to the apparent satisfaction of their employers. They were a disciplined and willing work-force – too disciplined and willing, some would say, not least in suffering the industrial illnesses, especially, common in such work. These workers – Pakistanis, Yemenis, Bengalis – were in origin peasants: very few had had any previous experience of industrial work. Similarly, the earlier generation of sailors came from a peasant background where it was unlikely any one had even seen the sea. Yet it is a common belief in many writings on industrialization that the transformation of peasants into workers is a protracted and difficult process, that peasants are lazy, uncontrollable people who have to learn to use machines and keep regular time. The classic instance of this is to be found in discussions of Russian industrialization both before and after the Revolution, where the resistance of ex-peasants to factory work is ascribed to inherent problems of a work-force drawn from the villages. The evidence of many ex-peasants in British factories, including Yemenis, conflicts with this thesis. It suggests that it is other factors, not least the manner in which the peasants are recruited and treated, not the work they are asked to do, which determines the degree to which they agree to do industrial work.

A 'Yemeni' Factory

Vivid illustration of these general characteristics of Yemenis in employment was provided by a visit in 1976 to a factory in Birmingham which, out of a total work-force of around 160, employed 100 or so Yemenis. The factory lay in the ring of industrial plans sitting in the valley that separates the Bullring and the centre of Birmingham from the nineteenth-century working-class suburbs that lie on the Heaths – Balsall and Small – behind, and where many immigrants now lived. The personnel manager of the factory had been with it for thirty years and explained that before then he had been in charge of an army engineering factory in Iraq, which had employed at one time 2000 Arab workers. As he explained, he had found them to be 'good workers': when in postwar Birmingham he had encountered a shortage of British workers due to the higher wages offered in the nearby Coventry car industry he had contacted the local Labour Exchange and asked them to provide Arab workers. Three Yemenis were sent to the factory, and the personnel manager never needed to go through the Exchange again. He recruited the other 100 workers over the next decade through these three. Talking to the workers and the personnel manager, it became evident that a classic chain had operated: many of the workers came from Dhala, and from one town in the North, and had obviously found work through informal channels of the usual kind.

The personnel manager seemed pleased with the performance of his Yemeni employees. Remarking that the morning shift began at 8.00, he produced the workers' time-cards to show that many arrived *before* 7.30. As elsewhere many Yemenis worked night-shifts; some night-shifts were composed entirely of Yemenis. But although there were three Yemenis on a factory council of six, the foremen in the factory were all English, despite the numerical predominance of Yemenis in the work-force as a whole.

The position of the Yemenis was in fact an extreme case of that of immigrants into European industry. Illiterate and unable to speak English they were isolated from British society and forced to take the worst and filthiest jobs; their colour and language separated them from society. But unlike the Pakistanis, Indians and Bengalis, with whom they shared the linguistic disability, they lacked the power of numbers of the larger communities. Where there were hundreds of thousands of South Asians, some at least would acquire the qualifications to become white-collar or skilled workers, or foremen, or to enter branches of employment other than industry. In the higher-income areas, there were also South Asian professionals and many with a working knowledge of English. A few Yemenis found in white-collar jobs – as doctors or local council workers – had come to Britain with these skills; none had emerged from the worker community. The Yemenis had no weight of numbers and no comparable skilled or professional sector to relieve their subordinate position. A few escaped to become shopkeepers, but these were the exception. The majority were at the bottom of the heap and likely to stay there; they were determined on the one hand to work as hard as possible to gain money for their families, and prevented on the other hand by a combination of factors from reaching a higher position on the occupational scale.

Housing and Social Conditions

In the 1960s and 1970s Yemeni immigrants lived in areas inhabited by larger communities of immigrants in some of England's larger cities. The main such areas were Birmingham (the Balsall Heath and Small Heath); Sheffield and Rotherham (Attercliffe and Burngreave); and Manchester (Eccles). When the Yemenis first came in the 1950s they lived as lodgers in crowded houses that were often in a decayed condition. 'We lived as many as eighteen in one house. Often someone had to sleep in the toilet,' a Sheffield worker told me. These conditions of atrocious housing in depressed urban areas were characteristic of other immigrants too, and the problems encountered by Yemenis were shared by Pakistanis, Irish and West Indians in the period.[10] By the mid 1960s, however, the situation had begun to change. Whereas in Cardiff and in South Shields the Yemenis were rehoused by the local councils as part of an urban redevelopment plan, the pattern was different in the industrial towns: here the Yemenis tended to buy their own houses. In the first place, they were not generally eligible for council houses, even had they wanted them, because, unlike the sailors, they were single men. Yet precisely for this reason, it was possible for two or three Yemeni wage-earners to get together and buy a house as a joint enterprise. Usually relatives or men from the same village, they would save and borrow to get the necessary deposit, then loan it to one member of the group who would formally buy the house. He, or in some cases a partnership of two men, could then collect money from the others in the form of rent, which would go towards paying off a mortgage. A typical two-storey Victorian terraced house in the Small Heath or Balsall Heath sections of Birmingham would cost around £2500 in the mid 1960s; the deposit might be £800 or about 30 per cent. Such a property was therefore within the grasp of regularly employed Yemenis, who might be earning up to £1500 a year.

By the 1970s, nearly all Yemenis in Birmingham and Sheffield lived in such Victorian terraced houses. Some Yemenis owned more than one house and rented the others out. Each man had his own room, and housekeeping was done on a shared basis. Individual men often cooked for themselves, and this fragmented cooking was made all the more necessary by the different shifts and therefore eating times of the men in the house. It was a common sight to see one man preparing his sandwiches for the night-shift around 6.30 in the evening, while another worker had just come home and was cooking his meal or sitting in front of the television eating the fish and chips he had bought on the way from the factory.

Yemenis bought a lot of their food from Pakistani butchers and grocers, who provided *halal* meat (killed according to Muslim stipulations) and the spices and vegetables used in Yemeni cooking. Lamb and tomato stew, with a good dose of cumin, was the basic Yemeni meal. They brewed strong cups of tea, of which a lot is drunk in Yemen, too; here, at least, Yemeni and British working-class habits coincide. A curious detail of Yemeni catering was the role of the half dozen or so Yemeni butchers who worked in each of the main cities. They travelled around the workers' houses in the daytime, and had duplicate sets of keys to let themselves in. The workers – either asleep after the night-shift or out at work – left their orders on a slip of paper, and the butchers put the meat, as requested, in the refrigerators to await the workers' return. The butcher collected the money once a week or whenever agreed. For such a practice to work there obviously had to be a strong element of trust on both sides.

Although the decoration and furniture in these houses was basically that of their previous British occupants, some identifiable signs of the Yemeni origin of their present owners could be seen. In the living-room where the members of the house came together there was always something on the wall that indicated a Yemeni or Arab connection – a picture of a Yemeni leader or a postcard view of a town, such as Ibb or Ta'iz, sometimes an old photo of Nasser that may have been there for ten or more years, perhaps a calendar, often a year or more out of date, of an Arab airline or a local Pakistani retailer. In their own rooms the workers had pictures of their families and friends, of home towns, and of themselves on special occasions. At home, the workers also changed out of their Western clothing: when they relaxed they wore the Yemeni kilt [the *futa*] and the small, often embroidered, Yemeni skullcap [the *imama*]. As in homes in Yemen, it was customary to take off one's shoes before going into rooms where food would be eaten. The centre of most houses was the kitchen and living-room: here in between work periods and at weekends the members of the house would sit together and talk.

Yemenis visted each other at weekends and on holidays; the addresses of friends were given not by street names and numbers but by the name of the person who was known to own the house. While in the early 1960s Dahya noted that Yemenis did not visit pubs, this had changed by the 1970s. Some Yemenis did drink in public houses, and at weekends groups of Yemenis could be seen in favourite neighbourhood pubs alongside other migrant groups – Irish and South Asians. But the most common meeting place for Yemenis outside the home was in the Yemeni café, a handful of which could be found in the major areas of settlement. In the Attercliffe area of Sheffield for example there were two cafés on the Worksop Road – the Qahwa and the Unity: the latter's English title – Unity Café – is a meaningful variant on the Arabic sign outside which proclaimed it to be the 'Restaurant of Arab Unity' [*Mata'am al-Wahda al-Arabiyya*]. In these cafés there was Yemeni music on the jukebox, Yemeni food and bread: dishes such as *asid* (stewed lamb), and *hilba* (a kind of sweetish dough). The cafés served above all as places where Yemenis met and talked. Predictably, attendance was to a considerable extent influenced by region and political affiliation: those from the North tended to go to one set of cafés, those from the South to the others. This practice was a case of the migrants making use of a British institution since, while the Yemen produces its own excellent coffee, cafés of this kind were unknown in the Yemens.

The division between Northerners and Southerners also applied to residential areas. The pattern of settlement in the 1950s and 1960s followed a simple path. One man would buy a house in a particular street; when another house in the street came up for sale the person selling or the local estate agent would ask the Yemeni if he knew anyone who wanted to buy the house. Naturally, if the man did know someone it would most likely be someone from his own village, whom he would want to have living nearby. Once two houses in the street were owned by Makbanis or Dhalais it was only a matter of time before further immigrants followed. In Birmingham for example the Balsall Heath area was the one where most North Yemenis were found, while the immigrants from the South tended to live in Small Heath. Small Heath was a characteristically mixed immigrant area. On the Coventry Road, the main artery and shopping street, the signs of this diversity were clear: the Muslim Commercial Bank stood two doors down from the Allied Irish Bank. Across the road a paper shop sold brightly coloured pictures of the Sacred Heart of Jesus, while next door stood a carpet shop with small coloured hangings of the Kaaba, the holy stone at Mecca, in the window. Down the streets which run off the Coventry Road were lines of Victorian terraced houses with, in some of them, a dozen or so Yemeni-owned houses. Next door lived English, Indian, Irish or Pakistani families. In Balsall Heath a similar pattern operated. In one street there were eight Yemeni houses, all inhabited by people from the Ta'iz area, and, a rare occurrence, even the shop on the corner was run by a Ta'izi. In the Balsall Heath there was also a building belonging to the *Zawiya Allawiya*, presumably that studied by Dahya in the early 1960s: it served as a centre for the North Yemeni community, who retained their devotion to everyday Islamic practice more assiduously than immigrants from the South.

Not all Yemenis remained integrated in the migrant community. I walked around Balsall Heath with an official of the local community association, who brought me to a house inhabited by three Yemenis who had, as it were, 'fallen out' of the community. They were unemployed and lived in filthy conditions in a derelict house where even the toilet had ceased to function. They knew virtually no English and had no idea about welfare benefits. How did they live? 'An occasional five shillings from Allah' was how one man answered. In a sense they illustrated very sharply the fate of those immigrants who failed to establish themselves and who had no community structures on which to fall back: they had to fall very far indeed before they were caught by the social workers of the British community. But in another sense their condition illustrated the degree to which most of the members of the Yemeni community were *not* living under these conditions but had managed to build a stable life for themselves. Precisely because the Yemenis came to earn money and send it home, they were intent on getting and keeping permanent jobs. Newcomers were helped to get established and survive. After the initial years of hardship and confusion, most Yemenis had by the mid 1970s achieved a settled if difficult level of existence.

Women: Absent and Present

A striking feature of these Yemeni migrant communities was the absence of any but a few immigrant women. In other Asian communities, though the men had come on their own, once established they tried to bring their families too. Until the 1980s, the Yemenis did not. One reason was the distinctive character of Yemeni migration: although they worked in Britain for years they were only here, in their own minds at least, on a temporary basis. There were, however, additional factors that contributed to this. The early sailors lived a shifting life and many did not have families in Yemen. Most who were married had English or Welsh wives whom they met in Britain. The later emigrants faced a different set of pressures. The migration of Yemenis that began in the early 1950s was uniquely one of men: there was, and is, little migration of peasant women from North and South Yemen to other countries, whether other countries in the Arab world or beyond.

Apart from the influence of village custom, the absence of a tradition of domestic service was another reason why the 'pull' or demand aspect was weaker: in the Middle East there was little demand for women domestic servants from Arab communities. The women who migrated in Europe, for example, often went into domestic service, but in the Arab world, and especially in the Arabian peninsula, domestic service was until recently performed by adolescent boys and men, not women; and in the past, of course, male slaves were brought over from Africa to be servants in the richer houses. When women did start to be used as domestic servants, these tended to come from South and South-East Asia. Hence there was an absence in the Middle East of one elsewhere significant pull on women to migrate.[11] Other areas of employment were even more male preserves, and remained so.

Equally important were the very strong pressures within the home community for the women not to migrate. It was generally felt that once a wife and children left, the worker would not send his remittances back; the other relatives who benefited were therefore opposed to the wife going, since they stood to lose access to the worker's remittances. In South Yemen, moreover, it was government policy until the early 1980s to prevent the wives of workers from leaving, since this would reduce the flow of foreign currency into the country and loosen ties between the migrant and the home community. The temporary character of Yemeni migration was itself a precondition for the continuing ties between migrant and home country, and this in turn discouraged workers, formally and informally, from bringing their wives to Britain.

The general consequence of this was that in North Yemen in the 1970s there were whole villages where virtually the only males were old men and boys below their late teens. The women here saw their husbands only for a few months every few years. In Britain, this pattern led to a further distinction between the two generations of Yemeni immigrant. The first generation, who settled in Cardiff and South Shields, had married non-immigrant women, so by the 1970s there were second- and third-generation children of mixed Yemeni and Welsh or English origin. Very few of the second wave of Yemeni migrants married in Britain (though some lived for longer or shorter periods with English women, while retaining families at home), and there were, until the 1980s, therefore relatively few children of these postwar immigrants given the size of the second wave as a whole.

A few dozen Yemeni women did come over with this second migrant wave and there were also a few Yemeni women in Cardiff married to sailors or to sons of the first generation. These women remain confined to domestic work: in the mid 1970s, so far as I could discover, none went out to work. They had even less contact with British society than the men did, since it was customary for men in Yemen to do the shopping, and in Britain most husbands of Yemeni wives did it too. The Yemeni women rarely visited one another, and had no communal meeting place, since they did not go to the Yemeni cafés. They therefore had even less opportunity to learn English in even the minimal way that most male workers did. One worker, whose wife did do the shopping, told me that although she went to the shops she could not read the writing on the goods, nor could she read Roman numerals. She was therefore unable to know either the prices on the goods she bought or the numbers on the banknotes she handed over.

In some ways it would appear that by coming to Britain these few dozen Yemeni women had entered an even more restrictive context than the one in which they lived at home. The basic ways in which Yemeni women get out of the home and of domestic isolation – through work and visiting – could not be used here, and the women were therefore liable to be trapped in the house. At the same time, other restrictions remained in force. At meals the traditional Yemeni system still operated whereby the women prepared the food and, while the men and other guests sat and ate it, stood looking on. The women then ate what was left, and although the convention of offering large amounts of food – that is, enough food for two separate meals – to the first lot of consumers was still maintained this did not detract from the subordinate manner in which women were treated in such contexts.

Another indication of how little traditional Yemeni attitudes to women had broken down came when I visited a literacy class organized by a Yemeni workers' group. In one room were a few boys aged between six and twelve, who were studying with the thirty or so male adult workers in the class; the presence of the boys would seem to have indicated that there were Yemeni mothers and presumably some Yemeni daughters in the district, yet none of them were present. When I asked the organizing official why there were no women or girls there, he replied that this was because the organization had not been able to set up a women's literacy class yet. The implication was that if women were to be educated this would have to take place separately; and it was evident, from the fact that no such class had yet been set up, that it was not a priority of the community to provide a means for women to meet and study outside the home. There was discussion of a plan to collect money and build a social centre for the Yemeni community, within which it was explicitly hoped that there would be a place where Yemeni women would come and meet. But in the community's spontaneous interaction with British society and in its initial organizational activities women did not apparently find any means of escaping – from the double restrictions of Yemeni society and of an entrapped condition within an alien, industrial, Britain.

Social Problems: *Al-Tax* and *Haqq al-Qahwa*

Most studies of immigrants concentrate on the three seemingly most pressing problems they face: housing, education and employment. These are all areas in which racial discrimination had operated and continues to do so. But in the 1970s these were not the main concerns expressed by the Yemeni community. Once the initial years were over, Yemenis were able, as already described, to settle in older owner-occupied houses; only a few now lived in bad conditions or in houses where they paid exorbitantly because of their racial origin. Education was not an immediate issue for the simple reason that there were very few Yemeni children; in Cardiff where there were children of Yemeni fathers and British mothers the children all spoke English and lived in the Butetown area where racist forces were less powerful. Employment was to some extent still a problem and, with the recession of the late 1970s, was to become more so; but in the mid 1970s the Yemenis seemed relatively secure and had tended to help one another to find jobs and to converge on specific factories. At that time, most discrimination was found where immigrants tried to get jobs in the skilled or professional fields, and the Yemenis had in the main not done this. That they should remain so confined to the unskilled sector was itself an index of discrimination, but it is a phenomenon they did not, in the main, try to resist.

On the other hand, the Yemenis did have acute problems, the most serious of which was what they call '*al-tax*'. If one asked any Yemeni immigrant about this issue a flood of anecdotes, resentments and queries would emerge, as well as sheaves of correspondence with officialdom. The reason was that the Yemenis had tax deducted from their wages at source, and this was done on the assumption that they were single men. They were, however, entitled to claim tax rebates for all children under the age of sixteen, but since these children were in North or South Yemen the British tax authorities were often reluctant to believe what the workers told them. The tax authorities may also have demanded forms of proof that that it was difficult for a Yemeni to provide – birth certificates, affidavits by government officials. One worker remarked that he had received a signed statement from a village schoolmaster attesting that he, the worker, had a certain number of children. But the tax official had replied: 'We know Aden because we used to rule it. There are no schools in the countryside, so there can't be any schoolmasters.' When the worker tried to explain that, since independence, schools had been opened in the villages, he was not believed.

The consequence of this problem was that workers were sometimes owed several years' rebates, amounting to perhaps thousands of pounds, by the British state, and that they were involved in protracted correspondence with a not always sympathetic officialdom. The ultimate recourse for someone in such a situation was to go the law courts, but for a Yemeni worker this was an almost unthinkable course of action, involving as it did legal work, technicalities and the possible displeasure of the authorities. They did not do this, but rather engaged in further correspondence and worry, trying to get back the fruit of their labour and send money to the relatives for whom they came to Britain to work in the first place.

The other analogous problem the Yemenis faced was that of passports. Those who came in the 1950s came on British colonial passports issued in Aden. This included those who were technically British subjects, that is, citizens of Aden and the Protectorates, and citizens of North Yemen, who were allowed to go to the South, and in particular to Aden, to work. Britain left Aden in 1967, and South Yemen, in common with all other former British colonies in the Arab world, did not join the Commonwealth. The immigrants with British passports therefore faced a choice when their passports ran out. If they opted for British nationality, they might have difficulties at home. If they opted for Yemeni nationality, they might have difficulties getting back to Britain. They therefore faced four different possibilities, each of which involved a certain cost: British nationality, North Yemeni, South Yemeni, or 'alien' status.

A quite distinct set of problems had arisen around the various kinds of corruption to which immigrants were subjected. The need to bribe people is known in Yemeni Arabic as *haqq al-qahwa* (literally, 'the right of coffee'): it was in essence a result of the fact that the Yemeni immigrant was someone who had cash and was in a vulnerable situation. Those with power to grant him something he needed, both at home and in Britain, were therefore in a position to make him pay to get that something, whether he was entitled to it or not. In the course of the migration process there were many different points at which the migrant could be squeezed. Seven of them follow here.

1. In order to gain entry to Britain in the 1950s a Yemeni had to get a passport from the British authorities in Aden. If he came from outside Aden, as they all did, he could only get a passport by proving that he was a citizen of one of the Protectorates and this involved receiving a document, or *tawdhif*, from the local sultan or sheikh recognized by Britain, testifying that this man was one of his subjects. To get such a statement the peasant had to pay the local ruler some money, and both those who were subjects of the ruler and those who were not were able to get their *tawdhif* in this way. Interior rulers, who were quite poor, were able to make some money out of this: one man who came in 1954 told me he had paid four Maria Theresa dollars, another man had paid twenty dollars, yet another had given the ruler a couple of goats.[12]

2. These rulers would make visits to Britain, for holidays or for discussions with the British government on the future of Aden, and this would provide them with another occasion to collect money. They would travel up from London and sit in the house of one of the immigrants. There, those from their area and anyone who had received a *tawdhif* from them would be expected to offer a present – clothes, a small radio, some token of respect. In the 1960s an ironic situation had developed in Birmingham where some Yemeni rulers would come up to visit the BSA factory in Sparkbrook to buy rifles for use either against the Republic in North Yemen or against the guerrillas in South Yemen. They would then demand presents from their subjects, some of whom at

the same time were sending money to support the Republicans and the NLF guerrillas in the fight *against* the sheikhs and sultans.

3. On their return to their villages, the workers had to perform similar acts of submission: before going to their families they were expected to pay a formal visit to the ruler, and present him with a gift they had brought from Britain.

4. If the worker had to pay at specific points of his progress, his family was permanently exposed to extraction. In an impoverished rural society a local tax collector or ruler would see where the most readily available source of cash was, and that the family receiving it were in no position to protect themselves. There are innumerable ways in which a local official could make life uncomfortable for such a peasant family if he so wished: he could impose extra taxes, or block some formal application, or confiscate an item of property. The peasant family who had attracted this trouble because they a had a bit of money would have to pay to rid themselves of this difficulty.

5. The claims of *haqq al-qahwa* caught the worker even in the most mundane activities abroad. He might need his passport renewed, or a government certificate, or permission to spend a certain time in or out of the country. When dealing from Birmingham or Sheffield with officials or, through middlemen, with these authorities, the worker could be forced to pay a certain sum. In one case the sum of £70 was mentioned to me as the fee a worker would have to pay to get a middleman to forward his application to the embassy for a passport renewal.

6. Not all those who took money from Yemenis were themselves Yemenis; bribery involving migrant sailors and workers had always occurred but as the situation of immigrants in Britain became more difficult, and employment became harder to find, more British people also discovered that money could be extracted from those who were in a weak position. The most common form of corruption occurred at the place of work, where Yemenis were willing to pay to get access to jobs. In the case of the sailors, this involved paying a British official to give them places on ships, when the supply of sailors exceeded the demand. Once such money has changed hands – the sum of £100 was mentioned to me in one port – there was of course no guarantee that the sailor would in the end be taken on. In factories bribery was concentrated on the issue of overtime and night work: in one

court case in the late 1960s, a British foreman in Cardiff was sent to prison for taking money from Yemenis in a factory where he was allocating overtime and night-shift work.

7. Finally, there was the most publicized corruption aspect of immigration – illegal entry. In Britain the willingness of Yemeni workers to take the risks involved in illegal entry rose with the increasingly severe immigration restrictions imposed after 1962. A report in one British paper in 1976 claimed that up to six hundred Yemenis were in Britain illegally, and that they had paid between £500 and £1600 to corrupt Yemeni intermediaries to find them a job and enable them to stay here. But, as the paper also pointed out, these Yemenis were ignorant of British law and were kept in a state of maximum dependence by these intermediaries who made large sums of money out of them.[13]

The issue of 'corruption' is a difficult one, both in definition and in the manner of best dealing with it. The basic cause was the same as that of Yemeni emigration generally: the poverty of the country and the extreme need of the people for work. On the other side, there are those in both Yemen and Britain who are willing to use their power to grant Yemenis access to work so as to line their own pockets. In many of these situations the worker is not offering money or gifts for something illegal; ordinarily he is simply paying for something to which he was entitled – a passport, an official document of some kind – or for which competition should have been on an equal and fair basis – signing on a ship, overtime or night-shift work. Corruption takes different forms in different kinds of society: in more advanced societies it usually takes the form of people paying for something underhand to occur. In poorer countries, a peasant or a worker has to pay to receive even that to which they are entitled. In the South Yemen of the 1970s at least it appeared that these practices had largely been ended. One group of workers in Sheffield told me: 'There is no *haqq al-qahwa* any more. That is what we were fighting for.'[14]

Anxieties of the Mid 1970s: Racism and Economic Depression

In the mid 1970s the Yemenis, like other immigrants, were often the object of racist animosities in their encounters with British society. Usually, however, this was not because they were seen as 'Arabs': there exists a strand of anti-Arab racism in British society, but this was derived not so much from any awareness of the existence of Arab immigrants in Britain but from stereotypes taken from the Middle East. The Yemenis in Britain encountered hostility because they were seen as members of a broader immigrant community: just as the Yemenis in Cardiff in 1919 were attacked because they were seen as 'black men', so Yemenis in the 1970s were seen as 'coloured' or 'Pakistanis' of a generic kind.

Two decades on, Yemenis remembered how in the 1950s, when they first arrived, they were attacked by gangs of Teddy Boys, especially when they tried to use certain pubs and cafés. But this declined over time, especially once the Yemenis got their own cafés, and overt and violent incidents more or less ceased to occur. Instead a less visible but quite powerful system of passive segregation grew up, whereby different groups of the population kept to themselves. Immigrants were discouraged from going beyond certain barriers, and in their own way they were not concerned to seek out contentious situations. A discussion in the sitting-room of a house in Birmingham with ten workers in 1975 brought out the way in which this system operated. The English workers were polite enough, they said, except when they were angry or drunk: then they started cursing and calling the Yemenis 'bloody Pakkies'. Socially they did not mix much, although occasionally they had drinks together in the pub. One man remarked that if you had a drink with an English worker a few times, one got the impression his workmates got at him about it and he would then pretend not to know the Yemeni if they met again. I asked them if they had ever been to eat in an English home, and none of them had. Had any English person ever drunk a cup of tea in this sitting-room with them? 'Yes,' they said, 'the man from the gas company and the man from the electricity company who came to read the meters'. Anyone else? 'No'. Yet they had been living there for almost twenty years. Sitting in a pub in Birmingham with a group of Yemenis one noticed the same thing: Yemeni men sat with Yemeni men, Irish with Irish. The only British people with whom the Yemenis had close contact were British women who were living with Yemenis; but they had almost become part of the Yemeni community. They were individuals who had crossed a barrier, rather than indications that the two communities had drawn much closer together.

Precisely because they were assimilated to the broader immigrant community the Yemenis were aware of the general ebb and flow of racist sentiment in Britain. In the spring of 1976 the National Front was campaigning on a racist platform in the town of Bradford: there was no Yemeni community in Bradford, yet Yemenis in other towns were well informed about events there. Later in the year the Front started campaigning in Rotherham where there are some hundreds of Yemenis within the 5000-strong Asian community. Here the Yemenis responded by participating in demonstrations with other immigrant and British groups. All Yemenis felt the attack on the immigrant community as a threat to them, even though they feel somewhat less exposed in so far as they had not decided to make Britain their permanent home. While the mid 1970s were a time of generally increased fear of racism, it was also a period in which the depression of the British economy hit hard at the immigrant community. The Yemenis were hit especially hard in two ways: first, because the decline of the pound reduced the value of the money they were sending home to two-thirds of what it had been in 1970; and second, because Yemenis returning after their stay at home found that they could not get their old jobs back since the firm had had to make workers redundant or, in one case at least, had gone out of business altogether. This, together with the increased racialist activity, itself feeding on unemployment and economic difficulties, made for a general sense of insecurity. While there was not yet a recurrence of the overt violence on a day-to-day basis that had marked the 1950s, the community was apprehensive about what the future would bring.

Yemeni idiomatic parlance for someone who is doing well is to call them a *bahri*. Literally meaning 'of the sea', and thence 'sailor', it came in earlier decades to mean someone who was prospering in life. As one man in a Sheffield café put it to me: 'Back in Yemen they used to think we were all *bahri* here. Now they know about there being no jobs and about the racialists, and they know we are not *bahri* anymore.' The economic problems, the hostility, the sheer grimness of separation for years in a cold and often ugly environment, the dirty work which many Yemenis do – all these were necessary to provide money that was so desperately needed at home. But it was a life born of extreme need, not one freely or joyfully chosen.

1 *Above*: Yemenis arrested during the 1930 Mill Dam protests. In the middle, Sandy Welbury, Deputy Chief Constable, South Shields Police. (Courtesy of *South Shields Gazette*.) 2 *Below*: A Yemeni funeral in South Shields, probably 1936. (Courtesy of *South Shields Gazette*.)

3 *Above*: Sheikh al-Hakimi (left foreground) and Sheikh Hassan Ismail (right foreground) with unidentified municipal officials.

4 *Below*: British wives of Yemeni sailors, in ceremonial garb, receiving instruction in Islam from al-Hakimi, South Shields, mid 1930s. (Courtesy of *al-Musawwar*.)

5 *Above*: Yemeni sailors and their children, South Shields.

6 *Below*: Procession by Yemenis, including some in naval uniform, South Shields, 1950s.

7 *Above*: The Nur al-Islam Mosque, Peel Street, Cardiff, prior to the 1958 redevelopment. (Courtesy of Welsh Industrial and Maritime Museum.)

8 *Below*: At prayer at the Cardiff Mosque, 1950. (Courtesy of the Hulton-Deutsch Collection.)

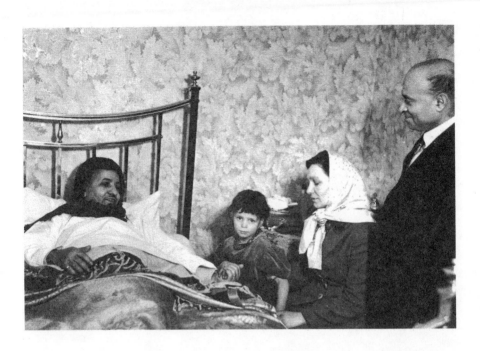

9 *Above*: Sheikh Abdullah Ali al-Hakimi (left) receives a Yemeni sailor and his family, Cardiff, 1950. (Courtesy of the Hulton-Deutsch Collection.)

10 *Below*: Retired Yemeni sailors at prayer in the South Shields Mosque, 1980s. (Courtesy of *South Shields Gazette*.)

11 *Opposite*: Yemenis in a Sheffield steel mill, 1990. (Courtesy of David Mansell.)

12 *Above*: Yemenis outside the Community Association, Burngreave Road, Sheffield, 1990. (Author's photo.)

13 *Below*: A Yemeni cafe, the 'Arabian Nights', Sheffield 1990. (Author's photo.)

14 *Above*: Yemeni teachers and students in the Literacy Campaign, Firth Park Youth and Community Centre, Sheffield 1990. (Courtesy of Iris Photography and Video Productions Ltd.) 15 *Below*: The Sanaa football team in Liverpool, 1985. (Courtesy of *al-Sharq al-Awsat*.)

Chapter 4

A Yemeni Workers' Organization

Nationalist Movements and Immigrant Activity

From the 1930s onwards, starting with al-Hakimi and *al-Salam*, there were political organizations among the Yemeni community in Britain. This chapter describes the workings of a union that was active among South Yemeni immigrants and the activities of its members in Britain during the 1970s. It was an exceptional organization, in comparison to those of most workers and immigrants: it was not a trade union in the sense of being directly concerned with the position of its members on the shopfloor, nor was it primarily concerned with the social situation of its members in *British* society. It was first of all an arm of the Yemeni state, an expression of Yemeni society and politics. It also reflected the fact that many of the Yemeni working class, from both North and South, were forced to work in exile. Their contribution to the development of their country and the manner in which their union was organized by the South Yemeni state to aid this development was a reflection of the underlying distortion of Yemeni society and the political forces this threw up. The reason why there were Yemeni industrial workers in West Bromwich was because there were no comparable jobs for them in Dhala and Ta'iz: it was in this context that the workers' organization among the Yemeni community defined its task.

The organization considered here in detail is the *Yemeni Workers Union* (henceforward YWU). This was founded in February 1970 and at the end of 1975, its peak of activity, it had an official membership of around 1900. In the late 1970s it became less active and in 1984 ceased to operate. The YWU was not the only organization within the Yemeni community, but it was the one with the widest range of activities and therefore most clearly illustrated the kind of work involved. A study of it is relevant to the general question of *immigrant organization*, since the YWU provides an interesting case of a successful and active organization among a body of migrant workers. The basic assumption of the union was that it constituted a link between the workers in Britain and their home country: it was consequently a reflection of the relationship between the migrants and their homeland, and tried to define the function of the British Yemeni community within the development of the home country.

There has been considerable debate about the disadvantages and benefits of emigration as far as the labour-exporting countries are concerned, and there is no doubt from these studies that the export of cheap labour to industrialized countries constitutes a net gain to the importing economies. However, neither the money sent home by workers, nor the skills acquired in the countries where they work, are usually put to proper use by the developing societies from which they come. In the Yemeni case, these general considerations operated, and there was always little prospect that the workers who had experienced work in the factories of industrial England would in the foreseeable future be able to contribute directly to the industrialization of their country. But the YWU, within the tight limits imposed on it, did try to maximize the contribution which the Yemeni community in Britain made to the efforts of those at home to overcome the historical backwardness of their country.[1]

Most analyses of immigrant organizations tend to concentrate on the relation between the immigrants and the community in which they have come to work. But this is far less important for Arab communities in Europe in general, and for Yemenis in particular. The Yemeni community in Britain in this respect bears similarities to the Algerian community in France: the most obvious point that these two communities have in common in the organizational field is that *it was not conditions in the country of work that determined the growth of their organizations, but the development of the nationalist movement at home that led to a mobilization of the migrant workers abroad.* For both the Algerians in France and the Yemenis in Britain, their awareness of the nationalist movement was all the greater because they were working in the country that was dominating their homeland and against whom the nationalist movements were fighting – from 1954 to 1963 and from 1963 to 1967 respectively. It was the launching of the FLN's guerrilla campaign against France in November 1954 that led to the growth of nationalist cells among workers in France: these contributed money and provided cover for political emissaries sent by the FLN to France. This also led to political actions by Algerians in France. In 1957 there was widespread support for an eight-day strike by Algerian workers against their French employers, and in 1961 Algerian workers supported the hunger strike of 421,000 Algerian prisoners of war held in France.[2]

There are two other features of the Algerian community in France which are comparable to that of the Yemenis in Britain. First, the history of the nationalist movement in France reflected not only the growth of, but also the divisions within, the nationalist movement at home. Prior to the FLN's campaign, a section of the Algerian community in France had been organized by the rival grouping led by Messali Hajj, and this rivalry, in some ways more open in France than in Algeria itself, continued at least until the FLN won independence in 1962. Second, following independence, there was a general expectation among the Algerians in France that the national government that had come to power would be able to find jobs for all those who needed them. Between 1962 and 1965 many Algerians who had been working in France went home in the hope of finding work. But this was a vain hope as the newly independent republic was stricken by economic and employment problems that made it impossible to absorb the potential labour-force. A decade and a half later, nearly 900,000 Algerians out of a total population of around 15 million still had to live abroad, 96 per cent of them in France.[3]

The Emergence of Political Organizations

The Yemeni community in Britain has always been numerically far smaller than that of the Algerians in France. It has therefore never played a political role in the UK comparable to that played by the Algerians in France in 1957 or 1961. But the history of the Yemeni community has been, like that of the Algerians, determined by the development of the nationalist struggle at home. As one leading official of the YWU in Birmingham put it to me: 'Our struggle here has been political – not social, or over working conditions. It has been part of the Arab struggles.' The first organization that had any stability amongst the Yemeni community was the Allawia Society, founded by Sheikh Abdullah Ali al-Hakimi in the late 1930s. Although first of all a religious organization, it had an important social role in organizing the community, and in the late 1940s, under the impact of events in North Yemen and in particular the Free Yemenis' revolt, it began to play a directly political role. This has already been described in Chapter 2, as has the manner in which this attempt, in some ways premature, to change a traditional grouping into a nationalist one, was in the end a failure. After the failure of al-Hakimi, the Allawia Society continued to operate; but while it still served a religious function, and while many more traditionally minded Yemenis still owed their prime loyalty to it, it did not play an active political role in the industrial centres where the second wave of Yemeni immigrants now live.

While there was a general sympathy among Yemeni immigrants for Arab nationalism and for the opposition movement in Aden in the mid 1950s, this did not at first lead to the growth of political organizations in Britain. Only after some years of trade union activity in Aden did an organization form in Britain; this tendency was then encouraged by the revolutionary overthrow of the imamate in North Yemen in September 1962, which led to the proclamation of a republic and to the eight-year civil war between republicans and royalists. The revolution in the North also led to a deterioration of the British position in South Yemen and in 1963 a guerrilla movement began in the Radfan mountains north of Aden. After four years of conflict, in both the mountains and in Aden itself, South Yemen gained independence under the leadership of the National Liberation Front.

Before discussing the impact of these later events, it is necessary to ask why the community reacted more favourably after 1962 than it had done to the events of 1948. The reason may lie in the character of the movements in the home country. The 1948 attempt against the imam in North Yemen was both secretive and, after some months, a failure. Its social base lay among merchants and intellectuals, and not among the peasantry from which the migrant workers were mainly drawn. The later movements were ones which mobilized thousands of workers in Aden, and which in North and South Yemen involved, after 1962, protracted military campaigns that were reported in the media and followed by the migrant workers through radio reports. They had a different social character and were more visible – and successful. The radio was very important as a means of arousing nationalist feeling throughout the Arab world in the 1950s and this was true, too, of the Yemeni community in Britain, who could listen to Cairo's *Voice of the Arabs* and its reports of events in both parts of Yemen. The migrants who came after the Second World War were also far more in touch with developments at home than were those of a more traditional outlook who had left earlier. They had close contact with relatives and fellow villagers in Aden and in the areas of military conflict, and were far less cut off than the sailors of the earlier period, who might in any case spend months at sea without any direct news of what was happening at home. By the late 1950s the working class in Aden was led by the Aden Trades Union Congress, which had organized several important strikes on a variety of economic and political issues. The first reflection of *this* kind of movement in the UK came in 1958 when a short-lived attempt was made to found a nationalist workers organization – the Yemen Workers Union. This claimed a membership of around 1000, mainly in Birmingham, but lasted only a few months; and it was only in 1961 that a more permanent organization came into existence, the Arab Workers Union [*Ittihad 'Ummal Al'Arab*]. This was Nasserist in outlook, in line with the nationalist movement at home, and was throughout the 1960s the dominant political organization among the Yemeni community. Once the 1962 reduction occurred, it won considerable support. Dahya reports widespread indifference among Yemeni workers to the AWU in the early 1960s, but the onset of the Yemeni civil war may even have changed that. AWU was the main focus of political work in support of the movements at home, and was at the same time the place where the increasingly sharp divisions within the nationalist movement at home were reflected, with splits between Ba'thist and Nasserist groups.

The first response of the Yemenis in Britain to the overthrow of the imam in 1962 was a tendency to support the newly proclaimed Yemeni Arab Republic. Out of economic optimism and patriotic interest, the Yemeni community in Britain, like Yemeni exile communities elsewhere, contributed part of their earnings and past savings to the newly founded Yemeni National Development Bank: within a few months an estimated £60,000 was deposited by Yemenis in Britain. This was, of course, a somewhat risky endeavour, given that Britain was fighting a war in Aden. On one occasion, in 1963, an inflammatory article in a British daily paper alleged that the funds being sent to North Yemen were being used to finance forces who had killed some British SAS soldiers in Radfan, on the boundary between the two states. As a result, the police in one of the larger industrial towns raided the homes of various Yemenis and took away papers. But, despite a constant stream of anti-Arab and anti-Yemeni commentary in the British press during this period, there were never any arrests or serious incidents. Later, during the four years of guerrilla struggle in South Yemen, a group within the AWU collected money for the NLF forces and transmitted the funds either through the NLF's offices in Cairo, or through individual couriers who were returning home on their temporary visits. At one time, around 500 workers were sending an average of £1 a week to the NLF.

In the late 1960s the AWU began to be affected by stresses within the nationalist movement as a whole. First of all, in South Yemen there was a split between the national organization FLOSY, which remained loyal to its original nationalist position and preserved close relations with the Egyptian state, and the NLF, which although similar in origin to FLOSY had developed along more radical and independent lines.[4] Second, while in the late 1960s the conflicts in the two parts of Yemen came to an end, they did so in strikingly different ways. In South Yemen, an independent state, led by the NLF, was established in November 1967, while in the North a coalition government uniting royalists and republicans was formed in the spring of 1970, bringing the civil war to an end. Third, within the NLF itself in South Yemen there was a running battle between two wings of the organization,

and only after 22 June 1969, when the 'left' wing of the party
gained decisive control, did there exist a more stable government
and clearer political line in Aden. By early 1970 there therefore
existed two 'camps' within the Yemeni movement – a camp led by
the NLF in South Yemen, and a camp loyal to the government in
the North, including former royalists, supporters of FLOSY, and
other republican elements. While it reflected the profoundly
different social situations in North and South Yemen, and while
each camp rallied its main support from those originating in either
camp, the division was more than just one between Northerners
and Southerners: when the split between the AWU and YWU
occurred in February 1970, each gained some support from people
originating in both North and South Yemen.

In the mid 1970s there were four distinct organizations within
the Yemen community, reflecting different aspects of the turbulence of the 1960s.

1   *The Arab Workers Union:* it continued to hold meetings on
    national and religious holidays, and to publish its magazine.
    Its main support came from workers originating in North
    Yemen and it was quite closely identified with the policies of
    the Sana'a government.

2   *The Yemeni Welfare Association [al-Djam'iyya al-Khayriyya
    al-Yamaniyya]:* this was a small grouping, based in
    Manchester, with an offical membership of 300. It or-
    ganized some meetings and regarded itself as an organiza-
    tion for helping migrant workers with problems they might
    have in relation to employment, passports or taxation.

3   The *Arab Workers League [Rabita al-'Ummal al-'Arab]:*
    this was based in Birmingham, and was especially strong
    among workers originating from the Makbana region of
    North Yemen. Its official membership was also around 300.

4   The *Yemeni Workers Union:* along with the Arab Workers
    Union was one of the most powerful and active groups
    among the Yemeni immigrants. Some of the work of the
    YWU, however, was also carried out by other groups,
    especially the AWU: they too held meetings on suitable
    occasions, organized literacy classes, produced magazines,
    and mobilized workers for Palestine demonstrations. Many

Table 6   Nationalist politics in Yemen and Migrant Organizations in Britain

Date	North Yemen	South Yemen	Britain
1948–9	Free Yemen revolt		al-Hakimi begins *al-Salam*, opposes imam's regime
1952			al-Hakimi leaves Cardiff, defeated
1955–6		rise of Aden trade unions, Suez crisis	Aden and Protectorate Association founded
1961			Arab Workers Union founded
1962	imam overthrown, civil war begins		
1963		guerrilla war begins	
1966–7		NLF–FLOSY dispute	disputes in the AWU
1967		independence	
1969		'left' NLF to power	
1970	coalition government		AWU–YWU division, Yemeni Workers Union founded

of the features and problems of the YWU's work can therefore be assumed to apply, to a greater or less extent, to these other organizations.

Function and Structure of the YWU

The YWU emerged from the AWU some time after the divisions which had caused the split in Britain had matured at home. One reason for this was no doubt the fact that it was not so much 1967 (formal independence) as 1969 (the advent of the 'left' of the NLF to power) which provided the basis in South Yemen for an initiative among the workers in Britain. A further reason for this is probably the fact that, as was also evident among the workers in France, delays occur between the country where the nationalist movement is fighting and the emigrant community that is supporting this movement. Unity may preserve itself in the exile community, after disunity has broken out at home. Conversely whilst reunification or reconciliation may occur at home, older animosities may survive abroad.

The YWU was founded at a meeting of eighty people in West Bromwich, Birmingham on 8 February 1970, and in the first issue of its paper *The Workers [al-'Ummal]* dated may 1970, the editorial asked, 'Why the Yemen Workers Union?' The explanation was:

> The establishment of the YWU in this country is intended, in the first place, to forge a link between the workers here and the workers' movement and the revolutionary socialist movement in the homeland, and therefore to transform work within the ranks of the workers and to increase their understanding of our Yemeni homeland and of the affairs of the Arab homeland and of the affairs of the Arab nation. . . . The reason for setting up this union is to serve the interests of the workers, even though this is a task beset with difficulties. We know we have few trained cadres, but we shall strengthen our work and we are serious about serving the interests of the workers. We shall build this union into being a true representative of the workers.

It is this 'link' which above all explains the work of the YWU. Politically and economically it was designed to provide support for the government in South Yemen and to the work being undertaken there in order to develop the economy. This was, in effect, a transformation of the pre-existing ties between Yemeni migrants and their homeland. The distinguishing characteristic of Yemeni migration was its 'recurrent' character or, put another way, the maintenance of the link between the migrant and his family and village. With the establishment of a government in South Yemen that was committed to mobilizing all available resources for economic development, the exile community took on a new character: their role was no longer to help those at home on a personal or family basis alone, but to contribute to the overall development programme of the society as determined by the state.

A clear statement of the YWU's outlook was given in a speech made by one of its officials at a conference of Yemeni emigrés held in Aden in 1971. The speaker declared that the establishment of the YWU was 'a true expression' of developments in the Yemeni homeland, and had come about after protracted political struggles. The YWU, he said, supported the 'progressive forces' in South Yemen and was building ties with progressive Arab groups in Britain and British left-wing groups. The speaker then went on to describe the contribution being made by the YWU to economic development in South Yemen: £7,000 had been raised for the 'Water Plan' then being implemented. Time and again in statements made by the YWU this theme of economic support recurs. For example, the political report presented to the third congress of the YWU in February 1976 stressed that 'the greatest achievement of your union has been its organization of support for the economic development plan, and its backing for the undertaking of the masses.'

The YWU's organizational structure was in a pyramid form, with at the base small local groups (*hayy'a*), above which was the district (literally region, *mantaqa*), and above this the section or area (*qism*). In the larger towns each section was made up of three or four districts, and in 1975 the nearly 1900 members were distributed as follows:

Section	*Membership*
Birmingham	800
Sheffield	750
Manchester	180
Newport	60
Liverpool	30
Middlesborough	30
Scunthorpe	20

A few other individual members were to be found in Coventry and some of the smaller ports. Overall, the strength of the YWU lay among the new immigrants in the industrial towns, with small supporting groups in the ports where the older communities lay. The highest body of the YWU was the congress, which met every two years, according to the constitution. After 1970, the YWU had held three congresses: the first in March 1970, the second in October 1972, and the third in February 1976. The third congress was attended by around 200 delegates and it elected a number of committees to run the YWU: a central committee of members, an executive committee, a cultural committee and an organizational committee.

A considerable amount of time inside the YWU was devoted to the discussion and co-ordination of the different branches and of reports on what was happening in the various locales. Routine as this may seem to be, the difficulty of such co-ordination can perhaps be appreciated by bearing in mind the limitations of the YWU itself. It had no full-time officials – all its members were voluntary workers, men who had jobs in factories. The fact that workers were often on Friday–Saturday night-shifts meant that members might not be available for discussions till late on Saturday afternoon. Even a simple operation like getting a cheque or letter countersigned by the three officials responsible could take one worker a whole evening. He had to take it around to the different houses, which might be in districts of Birmingham miles apart, and get it signed. Few of the workers were on the phone, and since they were on different shifts, the only time someone could be sure of getting them at home was in the early evening – or around seven in the morning. The problems of organizing members were even greater. They lived in different towns and a large percentage was illiterate; communications had to be by word of mouth and the convening of a regional, let alone national, congress was in itself a major organizational task, given the limited resources of the union.

Union Activities

Within the overall scope of the YWU's activities, there were five main aspects of its organizational work. These were:

1 fundraising for development projects at home
2 mobilization of support for political campaigns in Britain
3 convening of public meetings for the Yemeni community
4 literacy classes
5 publication of magazines

1. Support for development projects at home was the activity into which the YWU put its greatest efforts and the one of which it was proudest. It must be remembered that even in the 1970s the per capita income in South Yemen was under £50, and that at the time of independence there was not a single doctor or hospital

outside Aden in a country of 112,000 square miles. Adult illiteracy was over 80 per cent, and in the years immediately following independence the South Yemeni economy was further hit by the closure of the Suez Canal and thereafter of the British base in Aden, on which the prosperity of the town at least had been based. Four years after independence, in 1971, South Yemen began its first modest development plan, a three-year £40 million project, which was only partly successful because only about 65 per cent of the funds promised from abroad actually arrived. In 1974 a second, five-year, plan totalling £80 millions was begun; but South Yemen's vulnerability was evident in the period 1974–5 when it suffered badly from inflation in raw material prices and from heavy flooding which caused millions of pounds worth of damage.

As already mentioned, the YWU began collecting money for a plan to develop water resources as early as 1970, and within a year £7000 had been collected. In May 1973, a special Economic Development Fund was established by the union: YWU members were asked to contribute 50 pence a month, and this was later raised to £1 and then to £2 a month. On the wall of the YWU office in the Attercliffe area of Sheffield hung a photograph of a hospital, built at a cost of 31,000 dinars (about £50,000), at Shu'aib in the Second Governorate of South Yemen. The hospital was named the Hospital of the Three Martyrs, after three members of the NLF killed by a British mortar on 11 February 1967, on nearby Jabal Awabil. The hospital was jointly funded by emigrants in Britain, Kuwait and elsewhere: the YWU provided £5000 for a landrover and mobile medical unit sent off from Birmingham in November 1975. Other projects supported by the YWU included a road in the Yafai area of the Third Governorate, the establishment of various schools and cultural centres (*Marakiz Thaqafiya*) in the countryside, and schools for beduin (£2000 in 1973). The YWU also provided a contribution to the general fund of the 1974–8 five-year plan. In all, in the years 1973–5, the YWU Economic Development Fund collected £18,000 for economic development in South Yemen, of which £9800 came from Birmingham and £8800 from Sheffield.

2. The second major area of activity was mobilization of support for different political campaigns in Britain. In a significant statement in the political report to the third congress, it was stated

that 'The union will support the positions of all revolutionary forces in the Arab world and will be an ambassador of the cause of the Arab nation in this country.'

This political activity took the form of participation in demonstrations about relevant issues, the convening of meetings within the Yemeni community, the publication in YWU journals of articles on these struggles, and the provision of funds to causes supported by the union. The YWU always took an active part in the campaign to support the Palestinian resistance, and the YWU participated in demonstrations held in London on this issue. The YWU, and the other workers mobilized by the AWU, formed the largest group on marches backing the Palestinians and could be seen with their banners in Arabic and English massed around the podium from which speeches are made. During the October 1973 war, the YWU sent a sum of £7000 to the Palestinian resistance movement.

Another issue on which the YWU was active was support for the resistance movement in South Yemen's neighbour, Oman, where, from 1965 to 1975, a guerrilla war against the sultan was taking place. One worker in Sheffield told me how he had gone around his factory canteen with English-language publications of the Popular Front for the Liberation of Oman, trying to get the English workers to oppose the presence of British troops in Oman. He found little support from his work colleagues for this position, however. A third issue on which the YWU has been active is in opposition to racist activities in Britain. This is the one area of direct contact with other groups in Britain, with no connection to affairs in the Middle East. In Rotherham, for example, there were some hundreds of Yemenis among the 5000-strong community of Asian immigrants, mostly Pakistanis. During protests against the National Front in 1976, the YWU participated with the other immigrant groups and with some British groups in their campaigns.

3. The central means of mobilizing support among the workers was the public meeting held on occasions of national political significance. These were organized by all Yemeni groups and served a social function – as occasions to meet other workers – as well as a directly political one. There were three sorts of occasions for such meetings. In the first place, they were held on, or near, dates in the Yemeni political calendar that were also celebrated at

home: 22 June – the 'corrective move' of 1969; 26 September – the 1962 revolution in North Yemen; 14 October – the official beginning of the NLF's guerrilla campaign in 1963; 30 November – independence day in South Yemen, 1967. Then there were dates of more general significance in the socialist and Arab nationalist calendars: the first week in March – anniversary of the workers' strikes in Bahrain in 1965, and conventionally held as a week in support of the workers' movement in the oil states of the Gulf; 1 May – international workers' day; 9 June – anniversary of the start of the guerrilla movement in Oman in 1965; and Eid – the end of Ramadan, celebrated at different times of the year, depending on when it fell in the Muslim calendar. The AWU, but not the YWU, celebrated 23 July, the anniversary of the 1952 revolution in Egypt.

Meetings were also held when goverment officials were in Britain on visits or in transit from Europe or North America. Meetings of this latter kind had indeed been a long-standing feature of the Yemeni community. In the 1970s they took the form of question-and-answer sessions, between visiting ministers and groups of workers, on developments in economic, social and political matters. In the 1960s, leaders of the nationalist movement in Aden would travel to the Midlands when in London for conferences on the future of the then British Colony. In the 1940s and 1950s, sheikhs and members of the royal family from North Yemen would visit the workers and expect their obedient presence. All such visitors were, in different ways, aware of the economic importance of these communities: the difference is that in the 1970s it was people from the same background as the workers, and who claimed to be representative of their interests, who were coming up from London to talk with them.

Some of these meetings were held locally, but around half a dozen a year were organized as national meetings of the YWU. These tended to be held alternatively in Birmingham and Sheffield, with smaller delegations from the other towns coming to one or the other or both. On one occasion I travelled from Birmingham on a Sunday morning with three coachloads of Yemeni workers going up to the 1 May meeting in Sheffield. By seven in the morning, when most of the city was still asleep, dozens of Yemeni workers had gathered in the terrace house being used as a centre by the community at the time. Yemeni music was being played on cassettes, and as the buses drove through the deserted Sunday morning streets, the workers started singing about the then PDRY President Salem Rubbiya Ali – known by his followers as 'Salemin': *'Salemin, Salemin, Ya Mohibb al-Kadehin'* – Salemin, Salemin, Beloved of the Workers. One can only imagine what the few Birmingham residents then on the streets to get their morning milk and Sunday papers would have thought if they could have understood what these busloads of dark men were singing, attacking British imperialism and the perfidy of the Saudi ruling family. After the three-hour drive the busloads stopped for a couple of hours at a Yemeni cafe in Sheffield before going to the meeting at two o'clock. As well as being a trip to a political meeting, this was obviously also a social outing, an occasion to go to another town and to meet friends working there.

Sheffield Civic Hall, normally used for concerts and the conventional activities of such a centre, was on this day decked with portraits of the South Yemeni leaders, and with placards bearing slogans about the economic development plan and the need to fight 'Iranian expansionism' in the Gulf. In the entrance hall there was a picture exhibition of development projects in South Yemen. About 350 workers attended this meeting, and they sat packing the lower section of the hall. Such meetings were usually opened by a YWU official and there were then speeches by three or four officials of the union. These were sometimes followed by brief messages of greeting from friendly organizations – from local groups of Palestinian students, from Iranian students and from British groups working with the YWU on Middle Eastern matters.

In contrast to other political gatherings there were two features of these meetings that struck the outsider. The first was that, by conventional standards, the political speeches tended to be very short: there might have been one of ten to fifteen minutes at the beginning, but the rest were rarely longer than five and sometimes much shorter. The second feature was that after the political speeches the workers themselves put on various acts. There exists a popular tradition of Yemeni poetry and, in Yemen itself, it was usual to give recitations of poems. Among the Yemeni community in Britain, there were also some workers who wrote poetry, and they came on to the stage and read their poems to the meeting in a vigorous style. These poems tended to be about similar themes – their homesickness and their thoughts about Yemen, the work of the revolutionary movement, and the struggle for independence. Alternatively, there were performances by Yemeni comedians, who gave a deadpan stand-up performance in a Yemeni dialect incomprehensible even to the other Arabs. At the end there was often an Arabic film or, if there were visiting officials from home, a discussion.

It is evident that these meetings had an important social function, both formally and informally. Formally, this was reflected in the inclusion of poems, films and comic acts within the programme. Informally, it was clear from the fact that hours would be spent meeting and talking before the official business of the day began. Such meetings provided the one occasion when the Yemeni community in the UK as a whole came together in a coherent and distinct way.

4. The most important social activity performed by the YWU was the holding of literacy classes. Before independence there were few primary schools in South Yemen, and most of the population were wholly illiterate: in the mid 1970s the government in Aden had just begun a literacy campaign for adults, and adult illiteracy in the country was still high, at well over 70 per cent. Most of those workers who had come to Britain were also illiterate, and whatever else they had learnt in the UK, Arabic literacy was not one of them. Few learned to speak English with any proficiency, even though English words were incorporated into their Arabic speech.

The YWU had tried to run such classes for some years. A first attempt was made in 1970, but this was discontinued. A second try was made in 1975 and in 1976 there were six classes in all – three in Birmingham, two in Sheffield and one in Manchester. The classes tended to be from 2.00 to 6.00 p.m. on a Saturday, as was the case on the day I visited the three being provided in Birmingham. These were deliberately placed in different parts of the city, since one of the reasons why the early attempt had failed was that the workers found it an extra burden to have to travel far to get to the class. The first class, in the Sparkbrook area, was divided into two: one half was learning Arabic reading and writing, while the other half learnt English. On this occasion, there were nine worker-students in the class, and one teacher, himself a worker. The class was running for fourteen weeks and the full complement was thirty. The second class, in a school in

West Bromwich, had a group of fifteen worker-students and, in a separate room, a group of six beginners, three workers and three small boys. The teacher, Mohammad Saleh Qutaish, was a student of government at Birmingham University: orginally from the Ludar area of the third Governorate of South Yemen, he had previously worked on the staff of the prime minister of Aden. At a third class in the Halesowen district, there was a larger class of about twenty-five workers, with four young boys. Here, there were two teachers, both workers. One was an official of the YWU, the other was a well-known poet and singer within the Yemeni community. This class was studying four subjects: Arabic reading and writing, English, arithmetic and South Yemeni politics. For the Arabic they were using a basic textbook prepared for the adult literacy campaign in South Yemen – *We Read [Nahnu Nagra]*, a 224-page book which combined text, illustration and politico-social themes. For South Yemeni politics, they were using a short book prepared in South Yemen by the Ministry of Education.

The running of these literacy classes for Yemeni workers was a more difficult venture than it might at first appear, and these difficulties were not specific to the YWU: they cropped up in the literacy work being done among Algerian workers in France and were met by the other Yemeni groups who had tried to run these classes, including those co-ordinating adult literacy work in South Yemen. In the first place, there was a shortage of teachers. Some of the workers themselves were literate and hence could teach; but they were untrained and tended to use very traditional teaching methods. The largest supply of available literate Arabs in Britain were Arab students, many of them at universities or polytechnics in the towns where there were Yemeni workers. But the links between Arab students and workers were too rarely durable or close, and full use was certainly not made of this resource. There were, in addition, considerable problems in getting the workers to classes and even more in ensuring that they continued to come. As the workers worked on different shifts, it was often hard to ensure that those who came to a class one week could come the next. Those who worked a permanent Friday night-shift could not make it to a class that started at two on Saturday afternoon. As in South Yemen itself, teachers also reported that the workers who came expected to learn to read and write *too quickly*: after some weeks they felt that they had not made enough progress and therefore lost enthusiasm and stopped coming. On top of this must be added the particular difficulties of learning to read and write Arabic while in Britain. First of all, the learning in class was not reinforced: written Arabic was not a part of their everyday life and work; they had no chance to practise in the way they would have done at home. Second, the workers were deprived of the encouragement that comes (or may come) from participation in a widespread adult literacy campaign of the kind taking place in South Yemen. Where relatives, neighbours and workmates were involved in a campaign, and where the literacy classes were prominently reported in the media, there was a greater incentive to attend and to continue attending than there was in the already alien atmosphere of Attercliffe or West Bromwich.

Certain problems could have been lessened by outside help, either from local authorities or from other Arabs in Britain disposed to help. The hiring of teachers in English would have been much easier if there had been money to pay English teachers, and if a proper centre for the Yemeni community could have been built to which workers would come *anyway*, and not specifically for classes. It would also have been much easier for workers to attend classes if the factories in which they worked gave them day-release facilities. If the Arab student organizations in Britain had made it a deliberate and effective part of their policy to provide teachers for the workers, this too would have met the shortage of competent Arabic instructors. It was, in any case, an uphill struggle to teach literacy and other subjects given the accumulated cultural obstacles which the workers faced; yet if they had been provided with help of a kind that was modest in time and money and was consistently available, their work would have been that much easier.

5. The final distinct area of YWU activity was that of publications. Books and newspapers from South Yemen, from other Arab states and from Palestinian organizations were circulated among the workers. They also listened to Arabic radio – to Algiers, Cairo, and to the nearest audible Arabic-language radio of all, East Berlin.[5] However, the different organizations also provided publications of their own and after its founding the YWU produced *al-'Ummal [The Workers]*, a quarto duplicated magazine of around ten pages, with a printed cover bearing the slogan, 'On the shoulders of the workers are built the civilizations

of peoples'. Issue number 25, of May 1975, contained a characteristic set of contents:

- an editorial on the recently held sixth congress of the NLF;
- letters from South Yemen by YWU members spending time there;
- an article by YWU Secretary, Mohammad Abdullah Abdulilah, entitled 'A Great Triumph', on the recent NLF victory in South Vietnam;
- a review of a book by an Arabic journalist on the guerrilla war in the Dhofar province of Oman;
- news of developments in South Yemen.

Many issues also contain poems by Yemeni workers in Britain, or by popular poets at home. Issue number 23 of *al-'Ummal*, for example, contained two poems that had been read out at meetings in Sheffield and Birmingham to raise money for the development programme in South Yemen. *Al-'Ummal*, although supposed to come out every month, did not always do so, and this was understandable enough once it is remembered how overburdened the YWU was with its organizational workload. The magazine itself was produced on an old duplicator in the bedroom of one of the YWU officials: he and the other people in the house collated it, although on one occasion I saw it was collectively collated on a bus taking workers to one of the big Sunday meetings. The magazine, which was printed in 300 copies, was distributed among the community, roughly on the basis of one copy per house: it was reckoned that there should be one literate person there who could read it to the others.

A Political Orientation

Apart from these five areas of activity, the YWU had some contact with other groups in Britain. Its main relations were with organizations working in fields of direct relevance to it: on Middle Eastern matters, at a national level, or against racism, in local situations. While political speeches at Yemeni meetings sometimes reviewed the overall political situation in the world, and mentioned the role of the working class in the 'advanced capitalist countries', the YWU had little contact with British trade unions,

The **cover of** *al-Ummal* (The Workers), no. 25, 1 May 1975, price 3 pence.
The motto on the right reads: 'On the shoulders of the workers are built the
civilizations of peoples.' On the left it is stated that this is the organ of the
Yemen Workers' Union, United Kingdom, a branch of the General Union of
Yemeni Workers. Bottom left is the YWU emblem.

either at national or local level. Virtually all Yemeni workers belonged to a British trade union as well, and this was normally – since most Yemenis worked in engineering – the AEUW. But the Yemeni workers maintained a distinction between the two organizations: the British union covered matters of the shopfloor, the YWU carried on its quite separate activity. There was indeed a general feeling within the Yemeni community that the British unions neglected the problems of Yemeni workers and non-white workers generally. 'They just take our money and ignore us', was a typical comment. The YWU had no significant contact with British unions: its invitation to the TUC to send a delegate to the third congress of the YWU in 1976 did not receive a reply.

The YWU had additional reasons for avoiding any intervention on the shopfloor. All Yemenis were aware of the fact that as immigrants they were in an exposed position: the racist outbursts that occurred in British towns, and the campaigns against some Arab workers in Europe (Algerians in France, Palestinians in Germany) were followed closely and with unease. There was also the fact that, as one official of the Sheffield section put it to me, the YWU could not act *as a union* in any factory. In no factory was there a 100 per cent Yemeni work-force, even assuming that all the Yemenis there were members of the YWU. Moreover, the YWU had no strike funds: whatever it managed to collect it sent home for the economic development fund. In addition, there was an acute awareness that the reason they were in Britain was to help their families in Yemen: if the workers struck, their families at home would suffer, and there was no social security there to fall back on. The upshot was that the YWU had no presence on the shopfloor where its members worked. A handful of its members were shop stewards, but this was in their capacity as members of *British* unions.

What kind of organization was the YWU? It was not a *trade* union, since it was not organized on the basis of a specific branch of employment. Nor was it a typical immigrant organization. These tended either to be based on a kind of organization existing at home, which the immigrants brought with them – religious and secret-society-type organizations, for example – or to be some kind of organizational attempt to help the immigrants settle and adjust to the new situation in which they found themselves. The YWU differed from the former in that the members were not in

the YWU when they came to Britain – it did not exist in South
Yemen or in the UK – and in the fact that the YWU was based on
a quite new kind of principle: it was a *workers'* organization, not
the expression of some traditional or cultural system existing in
the country of origin. The YWU differed from the latter in that it
did not engage directly with British society, but it did, on the other
hand, see its main role as that of building political and economic
bonds between the workers in Britain and the country they came
from. The YWU was something unique in the UK, a political
organization acting as part of a radical state abroad. The
organization of migrants was, from the perspective of the South
Yemeni government, on a par with that of workers, peasants,
women and students at home. The nearest equivalent to the YWU
was the Indian Workers' Association (IWA), founded in the late
1950s and at one time enjoying a wide following among Indians
in Britain. This was an arm of the Communist Party of India, and,
with the divisions in that organization, the IWA in Britain also
split. It differed from the YWU in the most important respect of
all, however, because the IWA was in political support of a force
in India that was in opposition, while the YWU was supporting a
development programme being carried out by the South Yemeni
state.[6]

The YWU was the product of three distinct features of Yemeni
history and emigration. The first was the fact that the immigrants
did not consider themselves permanent settlers but were, as they
saw it, in Britain to help their families at home; they still saw
themselves as belonging to Yemini, not British, society. Second,
through the turbulence of the 1960s, a socialist government had
come to power in South Yemen which explicitly appealed for the
support of workers at home and, by extension, abroad. Third, this
government had by the early 1970s begun a process of economic
development and social change (espcially in the field of education)
which the Yemeni workers in Britain both supported and, in the
literacy campaign, reproduced here.

The early and mid 1970s represented the high point of YWU
activities, and the third congress, held in 1976, was to be the last
that it was able to organize. Following this congress, the YWU
declined in influence and organizational coherence and by the
early 1980s it had ceased to operate in a coherent way. A number
of factors contributed to this. First, the recession in the

engineering industry from the mid 1970s onwards led to increased unemployment among Yemenis, and many then left to find work in the Gulf or in Yemen itself. Some of the main organizers of the YWU were among those who were so affected and who departed. Second, the apparent unity which the South Yemeni leadership had been able to maintain in the early 1970s came to an end in late 1977 and early 1978, culminating in the outbreak of factional fighting on 26 June 1978, in which President Salim Rubiyya Ali lost his life. This crisis in Aden itself had its impact on the YWU and on the community as a whole, and made it more difficult to operate. It was some time before, in the mid 1980s, and in a different climate in both the UK and the Yemens, a new generation of Yemeni organizations, based on close co-operation with local government, were to emerge and continue the distinctive phenomenon of social and political organization within the community.

Chapter 5

A Community in Transition: The Yemenis in the 1980s

Factors for Change: British and Yemeni

The period up to the mid 1970s was one that included first the establishment and consolidation of the roughly 15,000-strong Yemeni community in Britain and, later, the emergence – a reflection of political changes in both North and South Yemen – of two immigrant organizations in the UK: the Arab Workers Union and the Union of Yemeni Workers. The decade and a half that followed saw a rather different pattern of development, one that both weakened the position of Yemenis in Britain and led to new, more assertive, forms of social and political identity. If, by 1990, the Yemenis were fewer in number than had hitherto been the case, and were an even smaller proportion of the 'Arab', 'Asian' and 'Muslim' immigrant subgroups, they had also succeeded in finding new forms of organization and expression in a changed British environment. The explanation for this outcome lies in the impact on the Yemenis of a number of different, often contradictory, changes in both the UK and the Yemens.

The most obvious characteristic of the Yemeni community in the late 1970s and 1980s was that it declined in numbers: by 1990 there were believed to be, at most, 8000 Yemenis in the UK, 6000 from the North and around 2000 from the South. As had been the case since the immigration controls of the early 1960s, there was little new migration to Britain, with the exception of some hundreds of women and children who came in the 1980s as a result of the liberalization of emigration in South Yemen. In Cardiff and South Shields there had been no new immigration for decades. In Sheffield a survey carried out in 1988 showed that

83 per cent of the men had arrived before 1970. But in addition to this virtual drying up of new immigrants, a substantial number left from the more recently established communities. The main reason for this was the economic recession: this hit in particular the engineering sectors in Sheffield, Birmingham and Manchester in which most Yemenis had been employed. In Birmingham, for example, unemployment rose four times in 1979–83 and the West Midlands as a whole had the worst long-term unemployment of any region in Britain, with four out of ten out of work for over a year. In February 1983 there were forty-six people seeking employment for every available job. Many of the Yemenis who lost their jobs went to Saudi Arabia and other oil-producing Peninsula countries to find work, although they would have been very unlikely to find employment that used the industrial skills they had learnt in Britain. A smaller number returned to the Yemens themselves. The number of Yemenis in Sheffield was reckoned to have fallen from up to 8000 in 1972 to 2000 in 1990, and of those who remained around 80 per cent were unemployed. A similar pattern prevailed in Birmingham. Elsewhere, where Yemenis had found other forms of employment, as in the shopkeeping of the Liverpool area, or the longer-established communities in South Shields and Cardiff, the situation was less severe.

To this reduction in the size of the community, and the unemployment that prevailed among many of those who remained, were added two other significant difficulties. The first was the general deterioration in relations between non-white and white communities in Britain in the late 1970s and 1980s, a process in part the result of economic conditions. By the mid 1970s, as indicated in Chapter 3, Yemenis were already beginning to comment on the increased incidence of racist abuse and harassment to which they were subjected: seen by whites as 'Pakistanis' and 'Asians' they suffered similar attacks to other communities in this period. For most of the time, this was based on general racist hostility, but particular issues that included, or appeared to include, Yemenis also had their effects: thus at the height of the conflict over the author Salman Rushdie in 1989 Yemenis, who as a whole remained removed from this dispute, were the object of anti-Islamic abuse; during the Kuwait crisis and the Gulf war of 1990–91 Yemenis and Yemeni property came in for attack: the Yemeni community school bus in Sheffield was destroyed, and Yemenis cafés harassed.

These changes in British society, compounded by developments in the Yemen, served to weaken the position of the community's organizations. The period of the mid 1970s had been one in which the governments of North and South Yemen became increasingly secure and concerned to organize their emigrant communities.[1] They were also, gradually, moving towards greater mutual understanding, with the eventual goal of achieving Yemeni 'unity', that is, the fusion of the two states. This meant that the two communities in Britain, and the organizations representing them, began to reduce tensions between them and collaborate more on matters of common concern. In 1977, however, this improvement in the Yemeni situation was reversed: North and South Yemen were increasingly in conflict. They fought a border war in 1979 and were in low-level armed conflict for another three years. While South Yemen appeared to be relaxing political and economic controls over its population in the early 1980s, and made its peace with the North in 1982, it was then convulsed by a bloody civil war in January 1986 that severely divided the state and the party. The results of these tensions in the Yemen were felt in the British Yemeni community: collaboration between the Northern and Southern groups was difficult, and the two unions themselves ceased to operate as they had in the early 1970s. The YWU held no conference after its 1976 gathering, and by the late 1970s neither organization was functioning at an effective level.

In the course of the 1980s, however, there developed two countervailing trends, ones that did enhance the Yemeni community's relation to British society and its own sense of cohesion. The first was the growing interaction of the Yemeni communities with local, municipal institutions and the funding by the latter of a variety of programmes designed to bolster Yemeni community. Hitherto Yemenis had remained outside the ambit of local councils and their social and economic programmes: but with the rise of awareness within councils of their responsibilities and of the particular difficulties immigrants faced Yemenis found themselves for the first time able to deal with institutions in British society on a community basis. This involved the setting up of the Yemeni Immigrants General Union (for those from the YAR) and Yemeni Community Associations (for those from the PDRY) in a number of cities; the organization of educational and employment programmes; the investigation by local council officials of the social and economic problems of Yemenis; and the involvement of Yemenis in the work of recording local, including immigrant, history. The result was that, despite the reduced numbers and the decline of the earlier political organizations, the degree of organization, activity and interaction with the surrounding society was greater at the end of the 1980s than at any previous time.

The other trend which positively affected the Yemeni communities in the late 1980s was the movement towards, and ultimate achievement of, Yemeni unity. The initial moves towards greater co-ordination of North and South that followed the ending of armed conflict in 1982 were, as already mentioned, halted when civil war broke out in the South in 1986. It appeared, at first, as if the two states were now set for another round of collision, one that would have had its effects within the community in Britain. Some months of tension did follow the 1986 crisis, but by 1987 a degree of trust had been restored between Aden and Sana'a and the process of building 'unity' relaunched. For a variety of reasons events then moved much faster than almost anyone could have imagined: by May 1990 it had become possible to proclaim the unification of the two states into a single Yemeni Republic, with its capital at Sana'a. The factors enabling this were several: the withdrawal of Soviet support for the South weakened the PDRY leadership's ability to continue as a separate, 'socialist-orientated', state; continued friction between the YAR and Saudi Arabia encouraged Northern President Ali Abdullah Salih to seek to bolster his regime by incorporating the Southern army; both regimes faced economic and political discontent which they hoped to offset by achieving the popular goal of unity; in the era of decreasing cold-war tensions, neither the USA nor the USSR sought to dissuade their respective Yemeni allies from engaging in a merger that, until recently, they would each have seen as strategically ominous. As a consequence, and much to the surprise of many outside the Yemens, a peaceful and generally popular unification of the two states was brought about, creating a new country of around twelve million inhabitants. The effect of this on the Yemeni community in Britain was direct: there was greater enthusiasm for this new state and for the prospects it opened up of resolving difficulties Yemenis had long faced, not least in resisting pressure from Saudi Arabia; in organizational terms, unity in the Yemens meant unification of all previously separate Northern and Southern groupings in the UK. In each city where Yemenis were organized into community associations, separate bodies were merged, thereby overcoming divisions that had lasted ever since the splits in the Yemeni nationalist movement thirty years before.

A Community Revitalized: The Case of Sheffield

The Yemeni community in Sheffield in the early part of 1990 presented a revealing picture of how these conflicting processes had affected what had been one of the largest of the postwar centres of Yemeni settlement. Sheffield had been one of the centres of the British steel industry and had, as a result, attracted substantial Third World immigration during the postwar boom. Sheffield had a comparatively smaller black community than any other major British city, but this amounted in the late 1980s to a total of around 30,000 out of a city population of around 525,000. Of these around half were South Asians, mainly Bengalis, another 37 per cent or so Afro-Caribbeans, and the remaining 13 per cent a combination of Yemenis, Somalis and Chinese. The Yemeni community had stood at around 8000 in the 1960s, at the moment when unskilled worker immigration had been stopped, but had been badly affected by the collapse of the steel industry in the early 1980s. As a result the community had shrunk by three-quarters, to around 2000, 1000 of whom were adults and the remaining 1000 second-generation children. On the other hand, while male immigration had been stopped, a small number of Yemeni women, from both North and South, had joined the previously all-male community. In addition to around 30 British women married to Yemeni men, there were about 180 adult Yemeni-born women in the community, and another 250 British-born Yemeni girls.

It was possible to gain a more systematic picture of the community in Sheffield because of two developments which had, over the course of the 1980s, served to highlight the situation of the city's Yemenis and thus to register and address their problems. One source of information and organization was Sheffield City

Council which had, as part of its more energetic concern with immigrant groups and racism in the city, developed for the first time close links with the Yemeni community and with its two organizations. Under its sponsorship, a Yemeni literacy campaign was launched and training programmes for unemployed Yemenis were set up. As a result of the collapse of the steel industry, unemployment amongst Yemenis was running at over 80 per cent and it was proving more and more difficult for Yemenis without skills and without adequate command of English to find employment. This change in Sheffield City Council policy was encouraged and underpinned by the changes within the Yemeni grouping itself, and in particular the establishment of the new set of community organizations, the Yemeni Community Association, representing the South Yemenis, and the Yemeni Immigrants General Union, representing those from the North. Both received support from their respective governments and from the City Council, and formed part of the new network of community organizations that had emerged among the Yemenis in Britain, in place of the old, more expressedly political, groupings of the 1960s and 1970s. While retaining, until Yemeni unity in May 1990, a separate organizational existence, the YCA and the YIGU were able to co-operate and together ran the Yemeni Welfare Advice Centre and other community schemes.

Beyond providing funding for the work of the Yemeni groups, the Council had in 1988 carried out a survey of the Yemeni community, the first of its kind, which provided a unique picture of Yemeni life in Britain.[2] Of the 354 Yemenis interviewed, 52 were women. The great majority of the men had arrived before the end of the 1960s: 57 per cent in the 1950s and 25 per cent in the 1960s, but most of the women – 83 per cent in all – had come since then.

Virtually all the men had found employment in the steel works, and there was, as a result, a very high incidence of industrial injury. Apart from many cases of burns and broken limbs, this work, under conditions of minimal safety awareness, had caused serious damage to their hearing: indeed, in a survey by the Sheffield Occupational Health Project of 800 Yemeni men, up to 90 per cent were found to have hearing loss sufficient to enable them to claim compensation, and one in seven had such extreme damage that they suffered from a permanent ringing in the ears,

حقائق
عن مدينتك

من الذي يدير مدينة شفيلد؟

التعليم .

خدمات البلدة و التخطيط .

الماء والخدمة المجتمع .

الساكن .

العمل

ماذا سيحدث لهذا التخطيط ؟

إذا كان الكومن يريد أن تتحكم في نيب خروف البلدب و هذا خطب لأن الكومن لا تريب ان

ما هو العمل ؟

المجلس البلدي لتجديد معظم الغابي في بريطانيا كلهم ضد هذا الرسم و لأنه يسبب في

إذا كنت تريد أن تساعد المجلس البلدي عارضت هذا القانون فقط اتصل برقم التلفون

التعليم والنشاط الرياضي

الرسوم القيم ودار الكتب

التعظيم والخدمة العامة.

من اين تأتي النقود و الى اين تذهب ؟

SHEFFIELD

CITY COUNCIL

Arabic-language leaflet on social services provided by Sheffield City Council, with guidance on how to obtain benefits. Note inversion of total for social service expenditure bill, bottom right.

Table 7 Sheffield Yemenis; year of Arrival to UK, Male and Female

	Men	%	Women	
Before 1940	2	2	1	
1940–44	0	2	0	2%
1945–9	2	2	0	
1950–54	14	57	1	
1955–9	127	57	1	4%
1960–64	39	25	2	
1965–9	23	25	4	12%
1970–74	21	17	15	
1975–9	7	17	17	
1980–84	13	17	8	83%
After 1984	1	17	3	

(Source: Sheffield City Council, Yemeni Community Surveys)

known as tinnitus. Many of those interviewed complained about the neglect and discrimination they had experienced at work, in particular by the unions.[3]

As in the 1960s the Yemeni community continued to be located around the old steel-producing areas of Attercliffe and Burngreave: on the Worksop Road alone there were six Yemeni-owned grocery shops, five Yemeni cafés serving Yemeni food and acting as social meeting places, and five mosques frequented mainly by Yemenis. At the headquarters of the Yemeni Community Association at 68 Burngreave Road it was possible to see at first hand how the new energies of the community were being channelled. Since its establishment in 1985, at a meeting attended by around 380 Sheffield Yemenis, the YCA had directed its energies towards particular projects, supported by the City Council. One was the organization of a Yemeni Literacy Campaign under which twelve young members of the community, trainees in teaching English as a second language, worked by teaching English to other members of the community and at the same time spent two and a half days per week training at Sheffield Polytechnic. Seventy-one people were in early 1990 attending these courses. The YCA also organized on its premises a literacy class for older men. Among the younger people involved there was a marked enthusiasm for the projects, and interest in Yemen even from teenagers who had never been there. A group of Yemeni women had organized themselves to carry out a number of educational and leisure activities – English-language courses, computing, sewing, swimming, day-trips, sport, and Yemeni parties. Twelve of them had written a joint letter to the Yemeni Community Association requesting that the YCA use its influence to restrict the consumption of the narcotic leaf *qat* by men in the community. The motivation of the older men in the education programmes was, inevitably, less constant: as one teacher told me, many had begun the literacy campaign with great enthusiasm, hoping thereby to go on to acquire a trade with which to find employment, but the difficulties of learning to read and speak English had proved in some cases too great.

There were numerous other signs of the vitality of the Yemeni community at this time. Three nights at week, an Arab School operated for two hours each evening teaching the Arabic language and Islam to children aged between five and sixteen. While the ability of the community members to send home regular remittances had declined, there had been special collections, and after severe flooding in South Yemen in 1989 £2600 was sent to the affected districts from which many of the migrants came. Migration was much more difficult than in the past, but there was a considerable flow of information through videos and newspapers sent directly through the embassies in London. In March 1990 every conversation seemed to turn to the question of Yemeni unity, the long-proclaimed but elusive goal of Yemeni nationalism which was, to the surprise of many, achieved two months later. Beyond its work with the City Council, the Yemeni community had also established a link with Radio Sheffield. On Sunday evenings, together with a Chilean and West Indian programme, it broadcast *al-Rukn al-Yamani*, [*The Yemeni Corner*], a fifteen-minute programme in Arabic. In marked contrast to the light-hearted Latin American and Caribbean programmes, which ran on music and chat, this consisted – very much in the style of official radio at home – of lengthy, solemn communiqués on the latest inter-ministerial meetings to discuss unity.

The impact of unemployment on the Yemeni community in the 1980s had been dramatic enough, leading three-quarters to leave, and rendering the majority of the rest without employment on a long-term basis. But it also had its impact through sharper discrimination and through promoting the climate of heightened racist intolerance that, in common with other non-white communities, the Yemenis felt with particular force. As those interviewed by the Sheffield City Council in the 1988 survey had indicated, insults on the street and discrimination at work had been constant features of life in Britain since the immigration of the 1950s.

But in the 1980s two things changed. The first was that, while in the 1950s and 1960s unskilled Yemeni labourers with no knowledge of English could find work, this was no longer so in the 1980s: their lack of skill, and especially their lack of English, served to lock them out of new employment possibilities. According to the YCA, of 20,000 new jobs created in the years 1986–90 not one had gone to a Yemeni. The second impact of this new climate was an increase in physical violence against Yemenis themselves. In September 1989 a sixty-six year-old retired steel worker, Muhammad Musa Salih, died an hour and a half after being attacked, along with another elderly Yemeni, on a Sheffield bus. Salih and his friend were returning home in the middle of the afternoon after attending Friday prayers at an Attercliffe mosque, when they were assaulted by two white youths shouting 'Black bastard' and 'Get out you wogs'. The attack occasioned great outrage within the Yemeni community, led to protests by a local MP, and brought hundreds of Yemenis to the dead man's funeral – the first such demonstration of Yemeni community members since 1976.[4]

This racist incident was then followed by another, which equally affected the morale of the Yemeni community. On 8 February 1990, at about 7 p.m. a group of five masked men, shouting 'black bastards' and armed with hammers and crowbars, suddenly burst into the Yemeni-owned Metro Cafe, and in the space of less than one minute smashed windows, electrical equipment, a billiard table and furniture, as the people in the café fled. When I visited the Metro a few weeks later, the owner Abdulla Ahmad Nasir, who came to Britain from Beihan in South Yemen in 1961, and had opened the café in 1981 after losing his job at a steel works, was beginning to rebuild it as a restaurant. But he was pessimistic: following the attack on a Pakistani video shop in nearby Rotherham, people were likely to be less willing to visit his new enterprise. The attack had had a serious effect on his wife, who was pregnant and caring for a handicapped child. These racist incidents were by no means the end of the story. After the onset of the Kuwait crisis in August 1990, abuse of Yemenis for their allegedly pro-Iraqi views was common, and the minibus used by the Arab School was wrecked.

South Shields: Beyond the Recession

As already discussed in Chapter 3, the South Shields Yemeni community was, with Cardiff, one of the two oldest in the UK: originating with the maritime link to Aden in the 1880s, it grew until the 1930s, when it numbered around 1000 members at its height. Half a century or more later, the community retained many of its characteristics, based around the Laygate area of what is officially known as 'High Shields' and numbering about 300 members. Many Yemenis still lived in the council housing estate of Cornwallis Square, on a hill overlooking the Laygate area, and two boarding houses, in Brunswick Street and St Jude's Terrace remained, though the restaurant attached to the latter had been closed. There had been no new migration in the 1970s and 1980s, indeed none of any significance since the 1930s. Of the 1000 or so members of the community in 1990 only around 100 had jobs. But, as elsewhere, what appeared to be a process of decline had, in some significant respects, been offset by changes in the organization of the community and in the environment in which it found itself.[5]

The first signs of change were evident on the coastal road to South Shields from Newcastle. Two decades earlier this area, once a centre of the British shipbuilding industry, was in grim decline, its links to the outside world broken and its population hit by serious unemployment. The South Shields Yemenis seemed to be a stranded group, left behind and now isolated by the shifts in the world economy. In 1990 the situation had changed: there had been considerable new investment in the North-East, industrial wastelands were being redeveloped, the rate of unemployment had fallen. The past was no longer just a source of nostalgia and, as elsewhere, municipal action had helped to give the Yemenis a new self-confidence. At Corporation Quay on the Mill Dam, where sailors had signed on to ships for decades and where the 1919 and 1930 'Arab riots' had broken out, a plaque erected in 1986 explained that the Dam had been built in 1863–4, just before South Shields was declared a separate customs port in 1865. Presumably this set of shipping offices was the first sight that Yemeni sailors coming to South Shields had encountered. Nearby there was a new Merchant Navy Memorial, with a statue of a weather-beaten skipper at the wheel, and a four-line verse by the poet John Masefield. It had been opened by Countess Mountbatten of Burma in September 1990 and, without listing those who died, was reminiscent of that at Liverpool on which the names of hundreds of dead Yemeni seamen were inscribed: 'In memory of the thousands of merchant seamen who sailed from this port and lost their lives in World War II'.

The Yemeni community itself, although not increased in numbers, had also become more active. The opening in 1972 of the al-Azhar mosque in Laygate had provided for the first time a proper place of worship and gathering for the Yemeni community: within walking distance of the boarding houses and of Cornwallis Square, it served the conventional religious and social purposes. About 100 Yemenis and Somalis regularly attended the al-Azhar mosque.

A further step was taken in December 1988 with the opening, next to the al-Azhar mosque, of the 'Yemeni School for Arabic and Islamic Studies'. This school was financed 75 per cent by the Yemeni, Saudi and Kuwaiti governments, and 25 per cent by subscriptions from the Yemeni community. The South Tyneside Council provided £35,000 to furnish the school. It provided classes in the evening and at weekends for Yemeni and other Islamic immigrants in the area. The school taught English, Arabic, Islamic studies and art and had, after two years of running, around thirty students, boys and girls. What was of considerable importance for the Yemeni community as a whole in this area was that this enabled them to teach the Arabic language and Islamic religion to the younger generation and so ensure a degree of continuity hitherto unattainable. Reduced and unemployed it may have been, but the South Shields community was still able to reproduce itself as a distinctly Yemeni community within the broader British and immigrant environment.

In the street running parallel to one of the boarding houses stood the Souq grocery store: a sign in Arabic on the outside announced that it sold halal meat. Run by Abdullah Hassan al-

Hukaimi, a thirty-four year-old British Yemeni, born in South Shields, the shop sold a range of goods for the Yemeni community, including spices and the halal meat, but included a range of goods for a wider Middle Eastern and Mediterranean clientele: pistachio nuts, curry powders, and favoured vegetables, such as okra. Abdullah Hassan explained that, while he serves the Yemeni community in particular, his business is also sustained by Arab students at the nearby Tyneside Technical College. Abdullah Hassan said he does not speak much Arabic but had retained the Islamic faith and that his children 'had not wandered' from the community. It was the time of the Gulf War and the Yemenis in the Souq shop were well aware of the apparent conflict between the attitude of their government and people at home, who opposed war against Iraq, and the 'Free Kuwait' stickers that adorned the flats next to the al-Azhar mosque. This was, they explained, because the Kuwaitis and the Saudis provided funds for the mosque and the Yemeni school: South Shields was indeed not as insulated from world events as the marooning of its Yemeni community over five decades might have suggested.

In the Shadow of the Tower: The Yemenis in London

In the history of Yemeni worker settlement in Britain, London never occupied a major part. Although it was one of the most important ports in the UK during the years of the earlier Yemeni immigration, and while West Indian, South Asian and Chinese sailor communities did develop, there is no record of Yemenis settling there in the first decades of this century. During the riots which London, in common with other ports, experienced in 1919, it was Chinese not Yemeni sailors who were attacked. Why this is so is obscure: it may have had something to do with the destinations of ships that picked up crews in Aden, or the fact that London was not a port for loading ships with coal. As for the second wave of Yemeni migration and its avoidance of London, the reasons are more obvious: London did not have the kind of industrial employment that attracted Asian, including Yemeni, workers in the 1950s and 1960s. Yet this apparent absence of Yemenis among the great mass of immigrants to London, over half of all those into the whole UK, is not entirely accurate. From the 1940s onwards and into the early 1990s, there was a small Yemeni sailor community in the East End of London which, while reproducing many of the general features of the communities elsewhere, also had its distinctive characteristics. Quite separately, and dispersed in other parts of London, there was a community of some hundreds of Adeni exiles, professionals and merchants who left South Yemen after the triumph of the NLF in 1967: they had, apparently, no contact either with the Yemeni community in the East End, or with other Yemeni communities in Britain, being separated by social and political character, and for a long time not regarding themselves as 'Yemeni' in a nationalist sense.

The working-class Yemenis of London find a mention in one of the first studies of Third World immigration to London, Michael Banton's *The Coloured Quarter*, published in 1955. Banton writes:

> In a badly blitzed part of London, half a mile to the east of the Tower and close to the docks, lies a huddle of mean streets where some three to four hundred West Africans and West Indians have made their home. This is no coloured ghetto but a depressed working-class neighbourhood sheltering residents of many races and nationalities, and one with a past little different from its present.[6]

This community was almost entirely a creation of the Second World War; while there had been colonial settlement further to the east, in Canning Town, prior to 1939, the movement of Asians and other immigrants into this part of Stepney dated from the war itself, which led to the evacuation of many of the previous inhabitants and the moving in of some hundreds of 'coloured' settlers. They set up a network of boarding houses and cafés, with some support from the British authorities, who made it their business to keep in touch with these colonial subjects in conditions of war. While most of these newcomers were, as Banton indicated, from the Caribbean and Africa, there were smaller groups of immigrants from other British colonies – Malta, Cyprus and 'Aden', that is, the hinterland.

In total, this group, classed by Banton as 'Mediterranean', numbered 500, with Adenis being the smallest group. Commenting on the 'Adenis', Banton records that a high proportion were seamen and that permanent settlement had been on a small scale. The figures given for Stepney in the 1951 census may understate the absolute figures, because of under-registration and the fact that men were away at sea, but they give an indication of the proportions. Of the roughly 100,000 inhabitants of Stepney as a whole, about 1150 were colonial subjects, another 965 Commonwealth citizens, and a further 8500 citizens of foreign countries. There were over 500 Maltese, 150 Cypriots, 40 Somalis and 17 Adenis: the latter two groups, in addition to being numerically smaller than the other colonial communities, were also distinguished from all others, except a group of twenty-four from British Guiana, in having no female component.[7] Banton also discusses the religious activities of the immigrant communities and reckons that there were between 2000 and 3000 Muslims in the whole east London region, the majority being Pakistanis. The main place of worship was a house converted into a mosque in 1940: yet, here the pattern of differentiation by ethnic origin prevailed, since this mosque was patronized by the Pakistanis, while the Adenis and Somalis had their own place of worship, the *zawiya*. This was presumably similar to those in South Shields and Cardiff and was part of the network set up by al-Hakimi in the 1940s.

The total number of Yemenis living in, or based in, this part of the docklands was probably never more than a few hundred and with the gradual decline of the London docks in the postwar period their source of livelihood moved elsewhere. Yet a tiny grouping lived on there, and in 1990 there were still around fifteen Yemenis in the Stepney area, by which time they had been joined by much larger numbers of Somalis fleeing the civil war in their country. The centre of the Yemeni world was the shop of Hajj Ali Salih Berim, located between the Horns and Horseshoe pub and a branch of Ladbrokes on the corner of Cable and Leman Street, in the heart of what had been Banton's 'coloured quarter'. It was from here that Hajj Salih distributed the twice-weekly consignments of *qat* that he received from Ethiopia. In his ground-floor room stood three large refrigerators, filled with bundles of *qat*, in half and quarter kilo portions, wrapped in banana leaves. On the wall was a Yemeni airlines calendar, a picture of Mecca, a map of North Yemen, and a sign saying 'No Credit Please'.

Hajj Salih, seated on cushions, with some Yemeni, Somali and

Ethiopian visitors, explained that he recieved 40 kilos of *qat* on a Saturday and 30 on a Tuesday. Since the price for a kilo ranged from £24 to £30 this represented a weekly turnover of around £2500 a week. In the course of one hour on a Saturday morning four men came to buy *qat*. He was one of the four traders handling *qat* in the London area, and despite some harassment from the press, managed to maintain a regular business, aided by his wife, that distributed *qat* to those in the London area who wanted it: the small Yemeni settler community, the Yemeni diplomatic and commercial community, Somali immigrants, and those from the *qat*-consuming parts of Ethiopia. There seemed to be no demand from the Adenis elsewhere in London, since traditionally the middle classes of the port had not consumed *qat* to a significant degree. For most purchasers, a quarter of a kilo was not enough for a good chew: the Somalis liked the stronger Kenyan variety, the Yemenis and the Ehtiopians the milder variant from Harar. Hajj Salih supplied soft drinks to accompany the chewing process, but disapproved of the practice which had, he said, originated in Aden, of drinking alcohol with *qat*.

Hajj Salih himself had first come to the UK as a ship's passenger in 1956 and had worked in a Sheffield factory for £7 a week. He was, he said, cold and poor and came to London where he opened a café with the help of an Irishman called Barry. Barry lent him slot machines to bring in custom, and for many years he ran the Welcome Café, serving Yemeni food for the community around. According to Hajj Salih there used to be four Yemeni boarding houses in the Stepney area, but there were now only ten to fifteen Yemenis settled in the area. Five were living on their pensions, and another five worked as janitors. The association with Mr Barry had given Hajj Salih a positive impression of the Irish: 'The Irish are like the Yemenis,' he said. 'They built London, just as the Yemenis built Saudi Arabia. No wonder the Saudis and the English get on so well – they don't do any work.'

Unwelcome Attentions: 'Killer Drug' and 'Brides for Sale'

The 1980s were not, however, only a time of retrenchment and some consolidation in the Yemeni community: they also brought unwelcome attention from the press on two particular, and sensitive, points. This was not the first time that the Yemenis had been recipients of hostile press publicity – there had been the racist coverage of the non-white seamen's question in the period after 1918, the sensational accounts of gun-running in the 1960s, and that of illegal immigration in the 1970s. This time, however, the issues were ones pertaining not so much to how Yemenis interacted with British society, but to how people in Yemen themselves led their lives, and how these practices were reproduced in Britain. What was involved was the sale and consumption of the narcotic *qat*, and the practice of arranged marriages. This was not simply a case of a clash between 'Western' and 'Yemeni' or 'Islamic' values, since within Yemen itself there had been considerable debate over these questions and criticism, on broadly 'modern' terms, of the practices. Both *qat* and arranged marriages were subjects of dispute and change within Yemeni society itself, and within the immigrant community in Britain; but the manner in which these issues were publicly aired in Britain left little room for such dissenting Yemeni voices to be heard.

Hajj Salih's trade in *qat* provided, as we have seen, a focal point for members of the lower Red Sea community in London – Yemenis, Somalis, Ethiopians – but it also provided a reference for a degree of critical and sometimes hostile, coverage of the impact of *qat* on those who consumed it. Although legally grown in Yemen, and legally traded internationally, *qat* had long been a subject of controversy in the Yemen itself, on the part of Yemeni reformers and of the British colonial authorities in Aden. A similar dispute had occurred in Somalia. There were two reasons for this: first, it was blamed for its negative impact on health, in particular the fact that it led to malnutrition and hallucinations; and, second, it was said to have negative social effects in that large amounts of time were spent in chewing it, and because family incomes were distorted by the fact that men diverted earnings away from the families nutritional and other needs to the purchase of *qat*. Defenders of *qat* pointed out that like any drug it could be abused, but that its physical and social effects were rather less than those of other tolerated substances, notably alcohol and cigarettes, and that in bringing together people it performed a significant social function, much as did the café or public house. Prior to their departure in 1967, the British authorities in Aden had considered a ban on *qat* but had decided against it. The revolutionary regime that replaced them took a firmer line, and in 1977 it restricted its sale and consumption to the Islamic weekend, that is, from 2.00 p.m. on Thursday through to midnight on Friday. The ban was certainly enforced for a number of years and strict penalties imposed on those who violated it: but whether it was in overall terms beneficial was less certain, since many of those who had previously consumed *qat* now turned to the rather more noxious and costly consumption of alcohol. The government of North Yemen, by contrast, imposed no such restrictions and with Yemeni unity in May 1990 all limitations on the sale and consumption of *qat* in the South were abolsihed.

The emergence of *qat* within the Yemeni community in Britain dates only from the 1950s. *Qat* leaves have to be chewed when fresh, preferably on the day they are picked, and prior to the development of air links between Aden and London it was not possible for Yemenis in the UK to obtain it. They had to make do with powdered *qat*, or with English shrubs that had, allegedly, similar properties. This was not, for the Yemenis, a matter of great concern since, although they had been used to chewing the drug at home, it is not normally addictive and it was therefore quite possible for them not to have it without this causing them difficulties. At some point in the 1950s, it seems, supplies of fresh *qat* leaves did become available in Britain when an Adeni businessman ran a DC-3 plane on the Aden–London route that brought in, among other things, *qat*. By the 1980s regular supplies were coming in from Ethiopia, where some of the highest quality *qat* is grown: it arrived on a twice-weekly basis and was within hours distributed around Britain by a network of rail parcel and van networks. On Saturdays in particular the bustle surrounding the arrival of the *qat* supplies was a familiar sight in Yemeni communities across the country.

There were those within the Yemeni community who were critical of the extent of *qat* consumption, particularly as the men in the community resorted to it more and more during the 1980s to compensate for unemployment and the lack of any plausible hope for the future. Those on unemployment beneift or pensions of £50 a week could use much of their income on *qat* – a good day's chewing could cost between £15 and £20. One did not have to probe far in the Yemeni community areas of the Midlands and

North to find the *qat* session: in dimly lit sheds, garages and top rooms they would gather in groups of six to a dozen in the afternoon and, seated on carpets and cushions, with the odd photo of Nasser or a Yemenia airlines calendar on the wall, they would pass the time chatting and chewing, with the television more often than not showing an Arabic video. For those from the North there was little resistance from within the community, but the policy of the Southern government that developed in the 1970s in trying to limit if not abolish the consumption of *qat* did have its echoes in Britain. The case of the twelve women in Sheffield, who wrote to the Community Association asking it to get the supply of *qat* stopped, was indicative of how changes of attitude in the Yemen itself were affecting the migrant community.

The public criticism of *qat* consumption in the UK did not, however, come from this source, but from parts of British society that became somewhat concerned by this phenomenon. First, there began to emerge a body of medical literature that highlighted potentially dangerous effects of prolonged *qat* chewing.[8] According to this literature, *qat* had been discovered to contain a stimulant, cathinone, similar to amphetamine; it could, under specific conditions, lead to paranoia and violent behaviour, as well as to various medical problems such as dental and gastric diseases, cirrhosis of the liver and impotence. The medical investigations were of cases where violent behaviour resulted and when the individual consumed *qat* on his own, that is, out of the normal social context in which consumption takes place. The experts writing these reports based their findings on a number of clinical cases, involving Somalis and Yemenis who had taken to violent action, and whom they had examined in hospitals in Britain. This medical literature did not explicitly call for a ban on *qat* but indicated that a prohibition might be desirable. One reason given for greater concern was the belief that the use of the narcotic was spreading beyond the initial immigrant group, to second-generation immigrants and to whites. In the words of one report: 'The possible need for preventive scheduling needs to be considered before an increase in the habit, particularly in immigrant groups, leads to problems'.[9]

A second source of anxiety about *qat* was the press. Sensational stories about *qat* had been published before, and this was perhaps encouraged by the general anxiety about drugs, and 'new' or 'exotic' substances in particular, that was characteristic of the 1980s. *Qat* may have been seen as even more strange because few who had not consumed it could believe that its effects were as mild as they really were. In October 1987, for example, under the headline 'Killer Drug Available for Sale in Britain', The *Observer* reported calls for an investigation into *qat* or, as the paper called it, 'khat' after a Somali refugee, whose mental state had apparently been affected while chewing *qat*, set fire to himself and a small child in the East End of London. At the inquest, a medical expert from the Royal Free Hospital reported that the man responsible for the two deaths, Abdulrazak Hassan Omar, had previously been in a psychiatric hospital suffering from paranoia and depression directly related to the chewing of *qat*. Beyond stressing the link between *qat* and paranoia in this case, medical opinion was quoted as suggesting that the incidence of *qat* consumption and hence of the inherent dangers were increasing. 'Khat is used as a relaxant, a sociable substance, if you like, in pretty much the same way as coca leaves were once used in South America – and look what's happened to cocaine,' said one expert. 'What's worrying is that we are seeing an increasing number of cases of psychosis which seem to be directly related to khat in this country.'[10]

The social and public concern about *qat* was even more evident in the third context – namely within the police. The legal and police situation with regard to any drug is, in part, a reflection of medical and chemical analysis of its likely effects, and in part a product of public concern: the police reflect and in some measure seek to respond to, or even pre-empt, what they see as public concern and adverse publicity. With the rapidly changing drugs situation in the 1980s, there was growing concern within the specialist drug units of the police force that the law was failing to take adequate note of a dangerous development. Several factors seem to have contributed to building up this concern, some of which were obvious: the growing body of medical literature critical of *qat*; the hostile press publicity; the ban imposed in 1989 by the US Drug Enforcement Agency on the import and sale of *qat*. But other factors also contributed to this increased concern. As hinted at in the medical literature, there was a fear within the police that the consumption of *qat*, hitherto confined to the Yemeni and Somali immigrant communities, was now spreading to cover sections of the white population as well. There was also a suspicion that the trade in *qat*, which was legal, was being used to cover the import and distribution of other substances, which were not. Here, as on the issue of other drugs, considerations conflicted. Concern to avoid adverse publicity for inaction was offset by the practical difficulties of monitoring the distribution of *qat* and by a desire to avoid creating another issue on which an immigrant, and particularly Muslim, community might be antagonized.

It was hard for those who sold and consumed *qat* to reply to this kind of critical attention. Public and press attitudes to drug consumption were in the main not only opposed to narcotic abuse, but tended to sensationalize where no danger existed, and there were too many cases of apparently innocuous substances having been found to have noxious effects for *qat* to escape easily. Yemeni migrants, with their long-standing fear of all publicity and authority, were unlikely to engage openly with such criticism. There were also, as already noted, those within the community who, while not necessarily favouring a complete ban on *qat*, did favour some restriction on its use and were concerned about its social and economic effects on the largely unemployed Yemeni community. Those who did defend *qat* tended to be people from outside the community who had knowledge of Yemen. One letter to the medical journal *The Lancet* questioned the assumption that *qat* had negative medical effects or that its social and economic consequences were exclusively negative. The letter also pointed out that if the existence of some negative consequences were to be used as a pretext for such concern, then other substances should also be examined: 'Before sounding the alarm on what is an important element of life for some sections of immigrant populations, it may be advisable to weight the evidence dispassionately, as we would/should do for ouzo, cassava, or maple syrup.'[11] *The Economist* provided another, more forthrightly entrepreneurial, defence. Indicating that *qat*'s bitter taste might be a selling point, it suggested: 'Perhaps they should market *qat* as an exotic health product. Look what the Koreans did for ginseng.'[12]

The dispute over *qat* could easily be seen as a clash between the concerns and values of the Yemeni immigrant community on the one hand, and those of the host, British, society on the other, as represented by the medical profession, the press and the police. In this it would have been no different from many other such conflicts between indigenous and immigrant communities in Britain and other developed countries. But the issue was more complicated than that: on the one hand, there was no one 'British' view on the subject – simply a number of views and considerations in favour of allowing *qat* to remain legal countering the pressure to control or prohibit it. On the other hand, the Yemeni community was itself not of one mind, especially when the long-running discussions within Yemen itself on the subject were taken into account. If this was true of *qat*, it applied equally to the other issue on which adverse publicity affected the Yemeni community, namely the practice of arranged marriages. This was a subject of frequent critical coverage with regard to South Asian immigrant communities; here too, what appeared to be a straight British–immigrant conflict of values in fact overlay a growing element of dispute and variation within the immigrant community itself and within the society from which the immigrants came.

As far as the Yemenis were concerned, the issue became a public one in 1986 when considerable publicity was given to the case of two British-born Yemeni girls who had allegedly been 'sold' by their father to husbands in Yemen. The two, Sana and Nadia Muhsin, were the children of a Yemeni migrant from Mukbana in North Yemen, Muthana Muhsin, and of a half-British half-Pakistani mother, Miriam Ali. The girls had lived in the Sparkbrook district of Birmingham until in 1980, at the ages of fifteen and thirteen, they had been sent by their father on 'holiday' to Yemen. They had not come back: once there, they had been told by relatives that their father had arranged for them to be married to local men. The 'marriages' had taken place and the girls, now women, had remained in rural Yemen ever since, where they now had children. Press coverage focused on several aspects of the case: the fact that the girls had not been informed about their father's plans before going to Yemen; the fact that Muthana Muhsin had received payment – £1300 – for the betrothals; the resistance of the girls to their 'marriage' – 'I screamed that I couldn't be married. My wedding night was rape,' ran one headline.'[13] According to the press reports, Nadia had tried to kill herself by taking an overdose of drugs, and both were desperate to get back to Birmingham.

The British Foreign Office was at first reluctant to become involved in what was formally a matter of purely Yemeni jurisdiction, since the two women were, by dint of their father's nationality, Yemeni. However, the British government did put pressure on the Yemeni government, at one point resorting to the practice of summoning the ambassador to the Foreign Office six times on a single day. In the end, after considerable publicity and comment, one of the sisters, Zana, did return to Britain in 1988 while Nadia moved from her village to live in the city of Ta'iz. Yet the underlying questions raised by this incident were not so easily passed over. For the British press who pursued this story it was simple enough − a brutal father, Muthana Muhsin, had sold and tricked his daughters in return for financial reward. The girls' mother, Miriam Ali, confirmed this approach, although she was to be unhappy about some of the methods used by the journalists who covered the story, and about some of what was said in the press. The father, who initially claimed he had done what he did to stop the girls becoming prostitutes and that the girls had known in advance that they were betrothed, later relented somewhat; but, with the support of many in the Yemeni community, he expressed resentment at the way the press had handled the story and 'distorted' the issues involved.

As with *qat* there were more questions involved than the hostile press or the defensive Yemeni reaction initially suggested. On one point there could be little doubt: whether or not arranged marriages were acceptable practice, they presupposed that the girls so betrothed had reasonable foreknowledge of such agreements, and the power to refuse if they did not want to proceed. This had certainly not occurred in this case: Zana and Nadia had been deceived, the father taking advantage of their being in Yemen itself to enforce his pre-arranged deal. On the other hand, as some subsequent discussion brought out, the image of such arrangements as being a form of 'human trade' was oversimplified, and distorted what was Yemeni convention. The practice of arranged marriages, and of paying a 'bridewealth' to the father of the bride was a common and generally accepted one in the Yemen. Some sought to derive this from Islam, others from Yemeni tribal tradition overlain with Islam. In either case, the core issue was not so much the 'arranged' character of the marriage or the paying of a 'bridewealth', but the question of choice.

Whatever the legitimation of its derivation from Islam, or south Arabian tradition, the arranging of marriages without the consent of the brides was beginning to be questioned within Yemen itself, and had, along with other forms of oppression of women, been strongly attacked during the revolutionary period in South Yemen. Indeed the hostile language used in British press coverage was, if anything, exceeded by that used during NLF campaigns in the South against the 'backward' and 'feudal' marriage customs hitherto prevailing. As one sympathetic but critical correspondent to the press wrote: 'It all smacks of yet another instance where the treatment of women is justified by way of a society's culture. Culture should be ever-changing and progressive.'[14] It was precisely this point that the deadlocked public character of the debate – one between British liberal values and Yemeni practice – seemed to obscure, since Yemeni society, at home and among the immigrants, was changing, if not as fast as many might have liked.[15] The result was that the Yemenis themselves tended to dig their heels in: in the face of what was seen as uncomprehending interference, Muthana Muhsin got the support of many men in the Yemeni community and many back in Yemeni itself. But others were not so sure: some years later, when talking to a British-born teenage Yemeni girl on a street in Sheffield, I asked her if she would like one day to visit Yemen. 'I would love to go for a few weeks,' she said, 'provided my dad came to fetch me back.'

In this, as in so many other issues, the development of the Yemeni community in Britain continued to reflect influences from both contexts – Britain and the Yemen. With the passage of time, the Yemenis remaining in Britain became more and more settled and the second and subsequent generations had a greater degree of assimilation into British life. Yet the gap between them and the mass of British society remained – as racist hostility and employment difficulties in the 1980s indicated – and the influence of the Yemen, both in terms of social tradition and political change, continued to be considerable.

Chapter 6

The 'Invisible' Arab

The preceding chapters have shown how, amidst a much broader flow of migration and economic change in the location and positioning of migrants, the 15,000-odd Yemeni community established and developed itself in Britain in a time-span running from before the First World War into the 1990s. The study began with a brief discussion of how Yemeni migration to Britain formed part of a much broader flow of Yemeni migrants, most of it to the oil-producing states and in particular Saudi Arabia, but a small percentage of it to industrialized countries, notably the USA. One obvious point of comparison between those who came to the UK and other Yemeni migrants was in terms of employment and position in the labour market. It was shown how migration to Britain, which located Yemenis at the bottom of the employment and social hierarchy, was comparable not only to that of other Yemenis to the USA, where they worked as agricultural labourers, heavy industrial workers and janitors, but also to that of the majority of Yemenis in Saudi Arabia, where they worked on construction sites. While some Yemeni migrants were merchants and traders, as in Saudi Arabia, Ethiopia, Singapore and Indonesia, this was the result of a distinct, anterior process, a nineteenth-century flow of migrants, many of them from the eastern, Hadramaut, region of South Yemen. The great majority of twentieth-century migrants were from the middle-western parts of Yemen, North and South, who became workers of one kind or another – sailors, agricultural and industrial labourers, employees of service industries. The British Yemeni community very much fitted this broader twentieth-century pattern, conforming above all to that of migration by Yemenis to the USA.

In this chapter, the Yemenis will be looked at in another comparative context, that of migration into the UK, with the purpose of identifying both those features of Yemeni migration to Britain that were common to that of other immigrants, and those that distinguished the Yemenis from comparable groups. The history and evolution of the Yemenis in Britain can be elucidated by looking both at what they had in common with other immigrants, and at what distinguished them.

Yemenis and South Asians: Characteristics Shared

Four features, in particular, of Yemeni migration to Britain are common to other migrant communities, and especially to those from the nearest and most similar region, namely South Asia – India, Pakistan and Bangladesh. The first and most obvious is the reason for migration, namely the desire to improve income and remit a portion of this income to home. To argue this is not to deny the importance of political factors in migration, and their contribution to the migration of Yemenis. A certain proportion of contemporary migration has been for political reasons – the exchange of Hindu and Muslim populations in the subcontinent in 1947–8 and the movements of Jews into and Arabs out of Palestine being examples. Political factors played a significant part in the great migrations to North and South America in the nineteenth and twentieth centuries. By the late 1980s millions of refugees were crossing frontiers as a result of wars in a variety of regions – Central America, the Horn of Africa, Afghanistan, Cambodia. Yemenis themselves often blamed migration, particularly that prior to the North Yemeni revolution of 1962, on political factors, and on the dictatorship of the imams, which held back economic development and discriminated against the population of the southern, Shafe'i, region of North Yemen. In reformist and nationalist perceptions of Yemen's plight in the 1950s and 1960s emigration was seen as one of the scourges visited upon the country by the Hamd ad-Din monarchy.

Clearly, in the case of Yemen, as in so many other cases, the political and the economic are not easy to separate: in so far as poverty and lack of economic opportunity reflected the character of government, its incompetence and tyranny, the migration from Yemen combined political and economic factors, as much as did the migration of people from Ireland after the famine of 1846, the latter being the result of British government policy. Yet in the sense in which refugees from civil war or victims of direct and discriminatory persecution were political refugees, those from Yemen to Britain were not. Once it is accepted that there is always an element of the political within the economic, then the causes of their movement can be seen as broadly falling into the latter category. This was something that the Yemenis held in common with the main groups of Third World migrants to Britain in the twentieth century and above all in the post-1945 period: Pakistanis, Indians, Bengalis, West Indians.

The second feature that the Yemeni migration shared with these migrants was that it was a form of 'chain' migration: this meant that the process of migration involved one person from a village coming to Britain and then arranging for others, relatives and associates, from that village to follow. In the words of one analyst of migration 'so long as there are people to emigrate, the principal cause of emigration is prior emigration.'[1] As discussed by Muhammad Anwar in his study of Pakistani migrants in the northern English town of Rochdale:

> Chain migration can be defined as the movement in which prospective migrants learn of opportunities, are provided with transportation and have initial accommodation and employment arranged by means of primary social relationship with previous migrants.[2]

The evidence of Yemeni migration conforms to this pattern: it was not a mass, simultaneous process, nor did the migrants move as individuals, finding employment, housing, location in an atomistic way. The first sailors travelled in groups, as gangs of twelve below decks, gradually settling in the ports and establishing their boarding houses, and then began to find employment on land. During the Second World War and afterwards they began to find employment in some industrial towns; they thereby formed the nuclei of the later communities. Time and again, in streets, workplaces, districts, the pattern of accumulation is clear, as those already established in Britain contact people at home and arrange for their passage. Once the new migrants arrive, they are housed, provided with a social context, and found work by those already there. In this way the new migrants are protected.

An attendant feature of chain migration is the belief that the residence in the country of immigration is only temporary. In the language of migration studies, those who come in this way are 'sojourners', not 'settlers'. The sojourner is not necessarily someone who actually returns, but rather someone who believes that he will return one day. As one analyst of Asians in Blackburn has written, the sojourner mentality is 'predicated upon a belief in the myth of return'.[3] This follows in part from the reason why such people migrate: they come to make enough money to return home, and then acquire a house and some land or other economic resource. Very often they do return home, once every three or four years, and most maintain the flow of remittances for considerable periods of time: but the majority were unable to return to work at home, and, while maintaining the idea of return, increasingly became *de facto* settlers. The departure of Yemenis from Britain in the 1980s was a result not of the fulfilment of the initial sojourner's expectation, that his stay would be temporary, but of the collapse of the employment upon which his initial migration and sojourning/settlement had depended.

This pattern of 'chain' migration helped to shape other characteristics which the Yemeni community shared with the South Asians. One is the way in which small informal networks of solidarity are established and maintained within the community. Mention will be made later of the religious and political groupings that were organized among the Yemenis; these had, however, a public and inclusive character. What underpinned the community were other forms of association that were more restricted and far less visible. Anwar's study of the Pakistanis in Rochdale identifies the extended kin networks known as *biraderi* [literally 'brotherhood'] which provided help with accommodation, transport, money, employment, and help at moments of special need.[4] The first thing they did, apart from providing money for the fare over to Britain, was to give the migrant an address to go to; years later the individual men would move out of their first place of residence, but the pattern identified by Dahya in the early 1960s, and still evident during my observations in the mid 1970s, was only gradually attenuated. Employment followed a similar pattern:

the practice identified among Anwar's Pakistani migrants, of 'ethnic work groups', that is, shifts of workers who all came from the same ethnic background, was also evident among Yemenis. This was exactly the practice followed by the Merchant Navy in its initial recruitment of Yemenis, with its policy of not 'mixing races below decks'. A similar pattern reproduced itself on land, where employers and Yemenis themselves often favoured ethnically homogeneous shifts in industrial work. The all-Yemeni workforce in the engineering factory discussed in Chapter 3 was a case of this.

The relationship of the Yemenis with the outside world, that is, the broader context of British society, was similar to that of the Pakistani migrants. On the one hand, the very strength of internal networks reinforced a process by which the migrants had restricted contact with the rest of society. This process, known as 'incapsulation', meant that for most of the necessities of life the migrant lived within an 'urban village' of his own people.[5] He lived in houses with others from his country or district, worked with them, handled social and religious activities in the same way. Despite the evident need of these migrants for forms of support in welfare terms, if only to inform them of their legal entitlements at work, they at first paid no attention to the policies of the host country, at either national or local level, with regard to social and economic matters. Thus it was not until the early 1970s that Anwar's Pakistanis began to apply for council housing. The Yemeni steel workers in Sheffield knew nothing of the payments they were entitled to for industrial deafness until their Community Association began pursuing the matter in the mid 1980s.

Most spectacular of all, however, was the linguistic consequence of this process: Yemenis who had lived in Britain for decades and who conducted their work and social lives apparently to their own satisfaction, could get by with only a smattering of English, a few words incorporated into Arabic, and a few phrases for engaging with the outside world. Employers would deal with their workforce through what Anwar terms the 'go between': the Arabic equivalent, the *muwasit*, was a familiar figure in Yemeni communities at home and abroad, and was responsible for a range of functions from transmitting money, to arranging for employment, to getting passports and visas sorted out. The picture painted by Jon Swanson of Yemenis in the USA is similar:

In America, the migrant divides his time among his home, his coffeehouse, and his job. Rarely is he without the company of his fellows in any of these situations; indeed, his life may be so insulated from the rest of American society that he can live for years in the heart of the city and gain no more than the most superficial understanding of the culture of which he is a part.[6]

Writing of Birmingham Yemenis, Dahya argued that if they were engaged in a process of assimilation, they could have been seen to challenge the indigenous population on three issues – jobs, housing, women. They chose instead not to assimilate, but to accommodate, in this way maintaining their separate identity and trying to avoid conflict by a process of voluntary segregation:

> The Yemeni migrants restrict their contacts with members of the host society to a minimum and fulfill roles which the host society considers appropriate for them; that is, the migrants do not appear – in the eyes of the host society – as competitors and therefore avoid conflict situations.[7]

One, initially paradoxical, aspect of this process of incapsulation as it affected the Yemenis was that it increased rather than decreased over time: the second generation of Yemeni migrants, those who went to Birmingham, Manchester and Sheffield to work in heavy industry, behaved in ways very similar to the Pakistanis; the first generation, however, were much less incapsulated in social and economic terms. The latter did mix with other nationalities and in many cases formed relationships with British women, and they also had much more contact with institutions of the host society, whether this be the employment offices for signing on ships or the local council in South Shields, which provided council houses for Yemenis in Cornwallis Square in the 1930s.

In employment, the common characteristics become more evident. Like the Pakistanis and Bengalis, the Yemenis were employed almost wholly at the bottom of the industrial hierarchy, working, quite simply, in jobs that the indigenous labour-force no longer wanted to do. This applied, in the Yemeni case, to work in heavy engineering, and especially to night-shift working. In Anwar's words, 'These were the sectors which had either lowest

pay or dirty jobs, difficult shifts and worst working conditions.'[8]
As has been discussed in Chapter 4, this was a common pattern
throughout the British labour-force in the postwar period.

The Islamic Dimension

The Yemeni migrants shared with those from Pakistan and Bengal
not only their motivation in coming to Britain, the pattern of
migration and settlement itself, and the working and social
conditions they endured, but one further defining characteristic,
namely their adherence to the Islamic religion. There is, however,
a need to be cautious about invoking this as an explanatory of
definitional concept, since it conceals a great deal of diversity and
interlocks with other, secular, forms of identity. In much of the
literature on the Islamic religion, equally in that produced by
Muslims and by non-Muslims, there is a belief that 'Islam' can be
treated as a single body of faith and that, more so than with
Christianity, its tenets and attitudes determine the lives of those
who adhere to it. 'Islam' is said to be all-encompassing and sets
the outlook of those who uphold it apart from the non-Muslim
world. Moreover, on the basis of this faith, Islamic migrants in
Britain share a common identity, such that they can be said to be
part of a 'Muslim community' in Britain. This essentialist,
timeless, all-embracing concept of Islam, found in earlier sociological and anthropological studies as in more recent writings, has
echoed hypostatizations emerging from the Islamic revolution in
Iran and such conflicts as that which erupted in 1989 over the
writer Salman Rushdie.[9]

There is, however, another way of looking at the relationship of
migrants to Islam and it is one which, applied equally to Yemenis
as to other Islamic migrants in Britain, may provide as many
insights as the more conventional total view mentioned above. All
Muslims do share certain tenets in common and in this minimal
sense there can be said to be a 'Muslim community' in Britain.
But, as with Christians, the unity ends there. First, there are
different shades of belief and patterns of organization: between
the Shi'ite merchants of Gujarati origin who came from East
Africa in the 1960s and the Bengali and Pakistani migrant workers
there is as much of a divide as between the Church of England and

West Indian Pentacostal churches. Moreover, while all profess adherence to a single religion, their religious practice in the migrant situation is to a great extent shaped by non-religious factors, by ethnic and sub-ethnic associations. Muslim migrants all go to mosques but the places where they choose to worship are chosen on a particularist basis: as was shown in a study of Muslims in Birmingham, the thirty-odd mosques there are attended by communities defined almost entirely, and divided almost entirely, along ethnic and regional lines.[10]

In the case of the Yemenis the same differentiations apply. The Yemenis who came to Britain were almost wholly Shafe'i Muslims from North and South Yemen and had therefore a common and distinct religious culture, not just vis-à-vis non-Muslims but within Islam itself. In an interesting break with the conventional pattern of reproducing the religious beliefs of home in the migrant context, in the 1930s and 1940s they were organized by Sheikh al-Hakimi, according to a quite different set of principles, into the *zawiyas*, inspired by the Allawi sect based in North Africa. But even though this was non-Yemeni in inspiration, it remained a separate, Yemeni organization: although with al-Hakimi's departure it lost its particular organizational coherence, the local *zawiyas* and the mosques that gradually replaced them retained a specific Yemeni character. Shared with Somalis in the first ports, these mosques were at first also used by the new generation of Muslim migrants from the Asian subcontinent. But over time separation occurred, so that by the 1970s and 1980s there were, alongside 'Bengali' and 'Pakistani' and various subdivisions of those groupings, Yemeni mosques. Many of the disputes which broke out in mosque communities in Britain in the 1970s and 1980s reflected, apart from administrative, personal and financial issues, differences between ethnic groups that had come together in the migrant context on the basis of supposedly shared values.

Below the appearance of Muslim universality, the migrants to Britain soon distributed themselves into religious groupings consonant with their ethnic origins. The most obvious reason for this was that since the mosque served a social as well as a religious function, immigrants chose to gather where they were most likely to meet people from their particular country, district or village. Moreover, as the story of Cardiff with its pro- and anti-al-Hakimi places of worship showed, even within the religiously and ethnically homogeneous Yemeni mosques subdivisions along tribal and sectarian grounds developed. If 'Islam' served, therefore, as in some measure a common characteristic that linked Yemenis to some other Asians, it did little to promote an integration or co-operation of the Yemenis with these others. Beyond the modicum of theological identity, ethnic and linguistic diversity prevailed.

The Distinctiveness of the Yemenis

Enough has been said to show how, across a wide range of national, social and economic issues, the Yemeni experience was in several respects similar to that of other migrants, those from Pakistan and Bengal in particular. In many respects, too, and despite the difference in the character of the host country, the Yemeni experience in Britain was similar to that of Yemenis in the USA. Yet this sense of the uniqueness of the British Yemeni community is not misleading and has been confirmed by certain specific features of the Yemeni migrant body that set it apart from other communities. Four of these distinguishing features are of special interest.

The first distinct aspect of the Yemenis was their history. The great majority of the Third World immigrants into Britain came after the Second World War: this was true of the West Indians and the South Asians of all kinds. None of these communities had existed before in any significant numbers. They came as passengers on ocean liners, and later by plane, and were employed in the new industrial openings of the postwar boom. The Yemenis, while caught up in this process, and employed in some of the industrial cities, had been in Britain since the First World War and had developed a network of residence, employment and collective organization well before these later immigrants arrived and settled. The organization of the Yemenis into the Allawi sect in the 1930s and the publication of *al-Salam*, al-Hakimi's paper in the late 1940s, the first Arabic or Islamic journal to be issued in Britain, was an index of this Yemeni advance on others. The Indian community, which numbered hundreds of thousands by the mid 1980s, totalled around 100 in 1939 and 1000 in 1949. Caribbean immigrants began arriving in 1948. In the 1930s alone there were several thousand Yemenis. By the late 1980s there were fifth-generation Yemenis living in Britain. Although later over-taken many times over by the numbers who settled in the UK, the Yemenis were the first significant Third World community to settle in Britain.

The second distinctive characteristic is their shifting identity in terms of how non-Yemenis perceived them. All people, and not least migrants, have multiple identities, born of the combined characteristics of where they come from and where they settle, and of the fact that everyone has multiple determinants – of place, region, gender, race, religion, nationality, political condition, and so forth. However, the degree of identity shift on the part of the Yemenis was especially marked and significant. This can be seen from the very wide range of terms used to identify Yemenis over the eight or so decades that they were present in Britain: as lascars, coloureds, blacks, negroes, Arabs, Adenis, Mediter-raneans, Muslims, Asians, South Asians, Pakistanis, Yemenis. Among themselves a different process of identification took place. None of these terms, except for 'Yemeni', was used, and that only with the development of a Yemeni national movement and consciousness in the 1960s; with the emergence of two Yemeni states, a process of classification took place, on the basis of which state they came from – 'Northerners' and 'Southerners' – but this never overrode the identification that had prevailed throughout the preceding years, namely one on the basis of their regional or 'tribal' origin – Shamiris, Shu'aibis, Makbanis, and so forth. This latter pattern of characterization was invisible to non-Yemenis, but only served to compound the tendency towards various identities.

The reasons for this multiplicity of identities were several. One was the uncertainty derived from the situation in the Yemens themselves: there, political nomenclature shifted over the years, so that even had those classifying the Yemens in Britain been in touch with the situation in South Arabia they would have altered what they said from time to time. What was originally 'Aden', became 'South Arabia', the 'Arab South', 'South' and 'North' Yemen and later 'Yemen'. Another factor was the pervasive tendency within Britain to lump the Yemenis together with some larger, more recognizable, group: thus the appelations 'coloured' and 'negro', used in the first two books on immigration into Britain, responded to this pressure.[13] So too did the various broader ethnic terms – Asian, South Asian, Arab, and so forth. In the 1980s the terms 'black', 'Muslim' and 'Yemeni' became particularly common, the former two in response to the trend within the home community, the latter in response to a new, more assertive Yemeni self-confidence.

The fluidity of identities accounts in part for one further striking characteristic of the Yemenis, namely their invisibility. An obvious reason for this was simply that there were not that many of them: 15,000 at most compared to hundreds of thousands of West Indians and South Asians. But the invisibility of the Yemenis had other causes as well.

One was the result of the shifting identities already mentioned: most of the time there was some larger identity into which they could easily be assimilated. In most cases there was an element of validity in this inclusion – lascars, Muslims, Arabs being cases in point. The characterization of them as 'Asians' or 'South Asians' was to some extent justifiable, but was not strictly accurate, since these geographical terms normally excluded the Middle East. The terms 'coloured', 'negro' and later 'black' were even more dubious, in that, in most political discourse, they applied to people of African or West Indian descent, although in the late 1980s the term 'black' did come to be applied to all non-whites, in particular to characterize those liable to white racist harassment. In some cases the Yemenis were simply classified in misleading residual categories – 'Mediterranean', in other words like Maltese and Cypriot, being one example.[13] Similarly, in areas where they lived near Pakistani migrant communities, it was quite common to see Yemenis classed as Pakistanis: this was as much the case for those who, in the racist idiom of the 1980s, abused Yemenis as 'Pakis', as it was for Pakistanis themselves who had to have it explained to them by the Yemenis that they could not speak Urdu or Punjabi as their interlocutors initially supposed.

There was, however, one further reason for the invisible character of the Yemenis or, to put it more accurately, for their remaining invisible until the emergence of explicitly Yemeni community organizations in the 1980s. This was, quite simply, the feeling on the part of the Yemenis that they would benefit from being as little noticed as possible. This was one part of the process of 'incapsulation' already noted, whereby immigrant community and host society together combine to insulate the migrants from the world around them. An obvious reason for this was the political culture, of clandestinity and caution, brought from the North and South Yemen themselves: they were used to conducting their affairs under the eye of oppressive and intrusive government; the concept of the state as having any 'welfare' function, or of being less than arbitary and remote, was alien. Another reason for self-imposed restraint was the fact that, while all were classified as British citizens, by dint of their coming from the protectorates of South Arabia, this was often not the case. Many migrants had come to Britain claiming to be from South Yemen, to be 'Adenis', when in fact they came from North Yemen: as explained in Chapter 3 they had paid a bribe to a British-protected ruler to say they were a subject of his. They did not want to draw attention to themselves or to their precise places of origin. If they were treated as Adenis or as generic 'lascars' that was fine with them. Political hostility to Arab and Yemeni nationalism within the UK compounded this. In the 1950s, the hostility in Britain to Arab nationalism represented by Nasser accounted for this, as did, in the 1960s, the fighting in South Yemen between British forces and the local guerrillas that preceded the British withdrawal from Aden in 1967.

The causes of this self-effacement were not merely political. The phenomenon of incapsulation certainly operated here. The lack of engagement by many Yemenis with the society around them, including with the welfare facilities offered by central and local government, is one obvious aspect of this. The almost complete confinement of Yemenis to the harsh industrial conditions they worked in meant that outside these almost unseen parts of the British economic landscape no one noticed them. But a further factor was the result of how Yemenis, with their long-established settlements in Britain, saw the newer immigrant communities and the assertiveness evident among them especially from the late 1960s onwards. Here there was often a suggestion on the part of the Yemenis that, in contrast to the others, they were not angry at British society and that they did not want to cause 'trouble' within it. They earned their income and maintained ties to the home country, but did not want to agitate for change. Here the 'sojourner' status played a significant part: the pervasiveness of the myth of return, of being temporary, not settlers, confirmed their relative reluctance to present themselves as a community.

This applied not only to their relations with British society at large, but to their relations with the two smaller communities of which they were members – the Muslim and the Arab. The latter, largely professional and middle-class Arabs based in the southern counties around London, knew nothing of or cared little for the Yemenis of the north and west. The former were very much concerned with their own, nationally defined community politics and religious practices and had little in common with the quite distinct Yemeni communities.

This relative invisibility of the Yemenis as far as British society was concerned contrasted with what is perhaps the most striking distinctive characteristic of the Yemenis as a whole: their unique levels of communal organization. Other immigrant communities had their religious, social and political organizations. The Indians had the Indian Workers' Association, which at its peak had a membership of some 20,000.[15] But no other migrant community in Britain had the degree of internal organization evident in the case of the Yemenis, and it is here that their contribution to the story of migration into Britain is most striking. In the 1930s, this took the form of the Allawi sect discussed in Chapter 3. In the 1960s there arose nationalist political organizations which included a majority of Yemenis within them, and, with the emergence of the two Yemenis states after 1967, these con-solidated into two blocs, one directed by the YAR goverment in Sana'a and the other by the PDRY state in Aden. As the analysis of the Yemeni Workers Union in Chapter 4 shows, this was a comprehensive political and social organization, directed at building and maintaining links with the home country and home state, and at pursuing among the migrant community in Britain the policies pursued by the state-run unions and 'mass organiza-tions' at home.

The explanation for this unique kind of immigrant organization lies both in the home country and in the British context. The reasons why the two Yemeni states maintained organizations of this kind were discussed in Chapter 4: these included economic factors – especially the need to keep remittances flowing – and political ones – the mobilization of support for the state, the exclusion of political rivals whether Yemeni or from other Arab states, and the monitoring of exiles' political loyalties. The question as to why the two Yemens, more than other home countries of immigrant communities, chose to promote immigrant organizations like the AWU and YWU lies in the distinctive political character of these states themselves, the particular paths of their revolutionary emergence and the anxieties they felt about political rivals from within Yemen or elsewhere in the Arab world recruiting or gaining ground among the immigrants.

On the side of the immigrant community itself, there is no single explanation. As the experience of al-Hakimi shows, there had already existed a history of organization, national and religious, within the Yemeni community, one that served both to link the Yemenis in Britain to the political campaigns of their homeland, and to organize the migrants around a number of particular welfare issues – literacy and religious education being the most obvious. At the same time, the very strength of the 'sojourner' mentality, and the limited contact with British society, meant that it was taken as understood by most Yemenis that their prime point of political and social contact was the home country, Yemen in one shape or another, and not the UK. The particular form that the 'sojourner' image takes is that, even when in many ways the links with the host country are far greater, including marriage and being of a second generation, there is a need felt to maintain the appearance of ties to the home country and so accept forms of association that preserve it.

This process of self-organization and linkage to the Yemen itself acquired a new character in the 1980s. For then, with the growth of encouragement among British local councils for ethnic associations, it was no longer so necessary to choose between Yemeni incapsulated organizations and assimilation into other, British, forms of association. Against a background of existing self-organization, the Yemenis were able to change what had been an incapsulated form of organization into one that had a direct, social, financial and administrative, link to British local government. The fusion of the two Yemens in May 1990 and the associated merger of the two immigrant associations strengthened this process.

In this, as in other respects, the Yemenis remained distinct. While forming part of the broader body of immigrants from Islamic countries in Britain, they maintained a separate organizational and religious structure, and were cautious about involvement in broader Islamic campaigns, especially when they saw these as manipulated by certain Islamic states, not least Saudi Arabia. The unions that evolved in the 1960s and 1970s had virtually no contact with British society or other immigrants: but the community associations of the 1980s built links between the Yemeni community and certain parts of the British state, rather than with other immigrants. Given the differences between their home countries and their home states, and given their long history of distinct self-organization, the Yemenis remained apart, as much in social terms as in evolving forms of distinct immigrant activity. In this, and for all the unacknowledged transition from sojourner to settler status, the British Yemenis constituted 'the remotest village', a self-enclosed urban community, one as remote from the British society around them as from life in the Yemen from which they came.

1. Correspondence Concerning the Building of Mosques in Cardiff and South Shields, 1938–9

(i) Letter of Sheikh al-Hakimi to the Governor of Aden, November 1938

Zaouia Islamia Allawouia Religious Society
OF THE UNITED KINGDOM

THE ZAOUIA
216, BUTE STREET,
CARDIFF.
26th November 1938.

To: Lt.Col. Sir B.R. Reilly, K.C.M.G., C.I.E., O.B.E.,
Governor of Aden.

Dear Sir,

I am writing you on behalf of the above Society, and also on behalf of the Moslems resident in the United Kingdom, thanking you for your letter of greeting.

Mr Brown spoke on the Wireless when we broadcasted, and we explained to him that we have purchased the ground to build a Mosque but that we now have not sufficient funds to carry on and build.

The lowest estimate that we have obtained is £4,000 and we should be obliged if you could use your influence in assisting us to raise this amount, either by public subscription or through a Broadcasted appeal.

There are a large number of Moslems resident in Cardiff, and many of us have become citizens, married, and have familys, and we are very anxious that our children shall be given the opportunity of being educated, and in this connection we hope to have your able assistance in raising the necessary £4,000 so that the Mosque and school can be built.

We have purchased the ground suitable to build on, for £500 but this has exhausted our resources, and as the men are seamen you will appreciate that it would take a long time to collect the necessary amount as there is a great deal of unemployment amongst seamen to-day.

When we commence to build we hope that you will lay the foundation stone with your name inscribed on it, and that will be a very happy day for us, and we trust for you.

We do not wish the money to be forwarded to us, but to be paid into the Bank, (National Provincial, Bute Docks), and I can assure you that our biggest ambition is to commence to build.

We should be glad if you will let us know if you can render us any assistance.

Salam Alaikoom Wu Rahmut Allah Wu Burakatto.

Sd/- Sheikh Abdulla Ali
President.

(ii) Report of BBC representative on visit to Cardiff, November 1938

On the 23rd November I attended on behalf of the C.O. the broadcasting of a programme by the Arab Fraternity at Cardiff. These Arabs are mainly Adenese seamen, and the B.B.C. had made an arrangement with them to broadcast their celebrations at the end of Ramadan.

The proceedings started quite early in the morning by the saying of Prayers in the Arab Clubroom. After this we proceeded through the streets to the Seamen's Institute where there were further Prayers and singing for a considerable period. After this the procession returned to the Clubroom and there were further celebrations. The whole proceeding must have lasted about two hours. At periods throughout the proceedings a broadcast was made by the recording van with a commentary by Sheikh Gomaa of the School of Oriental Studies, who assists the B.B.C. in their Arabic broadcasts. Mr Perowne read the letter from Sir Bernard

Reilly which forms the enclosure to No. 2 on this file, and the President, Sheikh Abdulla Ali, also spoke. These speeches were recorded for broadcasting.

The proceedings were interesting, and we were struck by the friendliness and smartness of all present. Most of the men were in their Arab robes and the procession made quite a picturesque sight.

After the proceedings were over, a Sergeant of the C.I.D. spoke to us and said that they had reason to suspect that Sheikh Abdulla Ali was carrying out marriages illegally. They think that he celebrates these marriages under Moslem custom without sending the married pair to the Civil Registrar for the marriage to be carried out under English law. If this is in fact happening Sheikh Abdulla Ali is of course liable to criminal prosecution. The Sergeant also said that he had heard that the Sheikh collected subscriptions from the Fraternity and, instead of banking all the money, kept some for himself. There may not necessarily be anything particularly remiss in this, as I understand it is a not uncommon custom! In view, however, of this information it was decided to cut out from the broadcast any speech made by Sheikh Abdulla Ali, and if there is any doubt as to his bona fides it will of course necessitate our being especially careful in handing over any money to the Fraternity for a Mosque.

I discussed this with Mr Perowne, and it is of course clear that if anything is to come of this proposal a body of trustees would have to be appointed and payments could only be made under the strictest safeguards. For the moment, however, the Society have been told that they must write a letter to Mr Perowne giving all details, and when he has secured the necessary information Mr Perowne will communicate with Sir Bernard Reilly in Aden. Then, if Sir Bernard Reilly thinks well, he can put up a proposal to us. The B.B.C have a certain amount of futher information. I gather that there is an Architect appointed, and a little money has been collected.

I believe that Sir Bernard Reilly mentioned this project to Lord Lloyd recently, and that Lord Lloyd thought it might be suitable for assistance by the British Council. No doubt when we get a recommendation from Sir Bernard Reilly he will mention this alternative, if he thinks it desirable to do so.

Meantime, I have received the letter at No. 3 from Sheikh

Abdulla Ali (forwarded to me by Mr. Perowne). I suggest that I should reply on the following lines.

'I have to thank you for your letter of the 26th November forwarded to me through Mr. Perowne of the British Broadcasting Corporation. As was explained to you in the letter from the Governor of Aden, which was read to you on the occasion of the recent broadcast, it would be best that you should first write a letter to Mr. S.H. Perowne at the British Broadcasting Corporation giving him full details in regard to the proposal to build a Mosque at Cardiff. He will then forward the information to Sir Bernard Reilly for his consideration.

This is the first step for you to take, and you will understand that it is not possible to give any promise of financial assistance. If, however, you will proceed as suggested, the question will be fully considered.'

(iii) Letter from Sir Bernard Reilly, Governor of Aden, to the Colonial Secretary, January 1939.

ADEN   GOVERNOR'S OFFICE
No. 17   18th January 1939

The Right Honourable
Malcolm MacDonald, M.P.
H.M.'s Principal Secretary of State
for the Colonies, 2,2Londonx.

Sir,
I have the honour to enclose copies of correspondence which I have received from the Arab communities in Cardiff and South Shields. The letter from Cardiff was addressed to me direct, while the letters from South Shields were sent by the Chief Constable with a covering letter, a copy of which has also been enclosed, to Mr. Stewart Perowne, who is seconded for service with British Broadcasting Corporation, and have been forwarded to me by him.

2. I understand that the majority of the Arabs resident in these two seaports are from Aden, the Aden Protectorate and the

Yemen; and, when on leave in England last year, I paid a short visit, accompanied by Mr. Perowne, to the South Shields community. Mr. Perowne also visited the Arab community at Cardiff, and in both seaports we were given to understand that these largely Adenese colonies were well-behaved and deserving people.

3. Both at Cardiff and South Shields, Mr. Perowne and I found that the main desire of these small Moslem communities was to possess Mosques, for which object they had collected among themselves a certain amount of money, but not sufficient to carry out their purpose. These Arabs work as seamen, but are liable to periods of unemployment, and their means are, therefore, very limited.

4. I should be glad if I could assist these Arabs in England, many of whom are British Subjects or British Protected Persons, and most of whom come from the south-western part of Arabia of which Aden is the natural outlet. If some financial assistance could be given to them to attain their desire for Mosques, I consider that this help would be very deeply appreciated not only by the immediate recipients, but also in the outside Moslem world, and especially in that part of it in which these people have their homes, namely Aden, the Aden Protectorate and the Yemen. Help to the cause of their religion, which is so dominant a factor in the minds of Arabs, would be useful in counteracting those influences which have been endeavouring to sow distrust between Arabs and the British.

5. The most practical way of helping these communities would be by contributing to the funds of the organizations responsible for the construction of the Mosques, but before any contribution was made from public funds the standing and integrity of the organisations must be examined. I fear that the results of such examination will show that they are men of small means and with no particular organising ability, and, however honest they may be personally, would probably be incapable of ensuring that none of their funds fell into the hands of unscrupulous and dishonest persons. I suggest, therefore, that it will be necessary to give practical assistance in the form of indirect supervision as well as by means of a substantial grant. This assistance could be given by having the local Committees properly organised and controlled, and I suggest that Mr. Stewart Perowne, with whom I have

discussed this question, might be asked to undertake this work unofficially. It will probably be necessary to consult the British Broadcasting Corporation, but I doubt whether they would raise any serious objection provided his work with them were not interfered with. The local Municipalities of Cardiff and South Shields might be asked to co-operate, and the local Borough architects could be asked to examine designs for the buildings and undertake the general technical supervision of the building work. It may be necessary to remunerate these gentlemen, and if this is so I suggest that the expenditure should be met from the grant to be made by Government. The actual building could be entrusted to a reputable firm of builders, and here again the co-operation of the Municipal authorities in advising would be of value. The funds should be deposited with the local branch of a bank of standing. The bank would probably undertake to act as treasurers.

6. In order to determine the amount of the grant to be made it will be necessary to examine the present circumstances of the two organisations which are interested in the construction of the Mosques. I suggest that Mr. Perowne be asked to visit both these centres and report on the present position and make recommendations.

7. As a considerable proportion of the Arabs in Cardiff and South Shields come from the Aden Protectorate or are closely connected with it, I suggest that the grant be accounted for as a special addition to the Aden Protectorate Budget.

> I have the honour to be,
> Sir,
> Your most obedient,
> humble servant,
>
> Governor.

[*Source*: Public Record Office, Aden: Original Correspondence, co 725/61/17, co 725/61/8.]

2. Sheffield Yemeni Welfare Advice Centre Constitution, 1985

Clause 1 – Name

The name of the organization shall be the Yemeni Welfare Advice Centre (hereinafter referred to as the "Centre").

Clause 2 – Purpose

1. The Centre shall seek to provide a comprehensive welfare rights service to Yemeni and other Arab speaking peoples in Sheffield.
2. In pursuance of this purpose the Centre may:
    a) provide for the supply of free and confidential information, advice and guidance.
    b) commission to be written and published any reports, leaflets or other relevant documents.
    c) arrange and provide the holding of meetings, courses and classes.
    d) organise and undertake relevant research work.
    e) receive monies or funds by way of donations, contributions and grants.
    f) affiliate to relevant institutions and organisations.

(N.B. "Relevant" shall be that determined by the Management Committee of the Centre)

Clause 3 – Management Committee

The Management Committee shall have the following membership:

a)   4 members elected by the YCA
b)   4 members elected by the YIGU
c)   4 members elected at the A.G.M.
d)   In the event of no representatives being nominated from either category (a) or (b) above there shall be 2 independent Arab speaking people nominated by SACG to sit on the Committee.

Clause 4 – Officers

Shall be elected from the Management Committee and should include the following:
   a. Chair
   b. Secretary
   c. Treasurer
Where possible, the Committee shall attempt to ensure that all the officer positions are not filled by people from the same community.

Clause 5 – Meetings of the Committee

1)   The Committee shall hold at least six meetings in each year. A special meeting of the Committee may be called by any two members of the Committee provided that seven days notice be given in writing to the other members of the matters to be discussed.
2)   The committee shall determine the number of members who shall form a quorum at meetings. The quorum shall be not less than 5.

Clause 6 – Annual General Meeting

1)   AGM's shall be convened by the committee at a venue acceptable to both communities.
2)   Not more than 14 months should elapse between AGM's.
3)   21 days notice of the meeting must be given by displaying notices in conspicuous places.
4)   The Chairperson shall preside at the meeting. In their absence the meeting shall appoint a Chairperson before any other business is transacted.
5)   All members of the Yemeni & Arab Speaking Peoples resident in Sheffield over eighteen shall be entitled to attend and vote.

6) The Committee shall present at each Annual General Meeting the written reports and independently audited accounts of the Centre for the previous year.
7) The AGM shall elect 4 members to sit on the Management Committee.

Clause 7 – Special General Meeting

The Committee may convene a Special General Meeting at any time and the provisions of clause 6 shall apply.

Clause 8 – Voting

Except where otherwise provided for in this Constitution every matter shall be determined by majority vote. Where there is an equality of votes the Chairperson shall have a second vote.

Clause 9 – Changes to Constitution

Changes to the constitution must be agreed by a 2/3 majority at an Annual or Special General Meeting.

Clause 10 – Dissolution

The organisation can only be dissolved with the agreement of a 2/3 majority at an Annual or Special General Meeting.

Assets will be divided between the YIGU and the YCA or transferred to an organisation with similar aims to the YWAC.

DB/IS 12th December, 1985.

Notes

1 Yemeni Migration and its Contexts

1. *The Economist*, 17 September 1988, calculated that the 500,000-odd Arabs in Britain represented about 10 per cent of all foreigners resident in Britain. See also Abbas Shiblak ed., *The Arabs in Britain*, London 1991.
2. For the early Lebanese migration see Elie Safa, *L'émigration libanaise*, Beirut 1960; and my 'The Arabs of Manchester', *British Journal of Middle Eastern Studies*, BRISMES, vol. 19, no. 2, forthcoming, 1993.
3. J. S. Birks and C. A. Sinclair, *Arab Manpower*, London 1980, pp. 244–65.
4. Minority Rights Group, *Migrant Workers in Western Europe*, London 1974.
5. See my *Revolution and Foreign Policy: The Case of South Yemen, 1967–1987*, Cambridge 1990, Chapter 4, for details.
6. Sydney Collins, *Coloured Minorities in Britain*, London 1957, p. 203.
7. Dorreen Ingrams, *A Time in Arabia*, London 1970, p. 88.
8. The Zeidis are part of the Shi'a branch of Islam, which is found in Iran and in some other parts of the Arab world; the Shafeis are part of the Sunni branch, which predominates in the Muslim world.
9. *MERIP Reports* 34, pp. 22–5, gives an account by Mary Bisharat of the Yemenis in California in the 1970s. The same issue also describes the Arab community in Dearborn, Michigan. For a later account see Jonathan Friedlander ed., *Sojourners and Settlers*, Salt Lake City 1988.
10. *Le Monde*, 31 October 1975, quoting YAR Yahya Jaghman, Vice-Premier and Minister of Economics.
11. Said el-Attar, *Le sous-développement économique et social du Yemen*, Algiers 1964, p. 65, quoting the Adeni magazine *al Fadhlul*, 26 December 1952.

2 The First Yemeni Migration

1. This account of Cardiff is largely based on K. S. Little, *Negroes in Britain*, London 1947. References here are to the 1972 edition, with an introduction by Leonard Bloom.
2. Howard Smith, *Heaven Lies Above Us*.
3. For general background see Conrad Dixon, 'Lascars, the forgotten Seamen', in Rosemary Omer and Gerald Panting, eds, *Working Men Who Got Wet*, St. John's, Newfoundland, 1980.
4. Little, p. 85.
5. Neil Evans, 'Regulating the Reserve Army: Arabs, Blacks and the Local State in Cardiff, 1919–1945', *Immigrants and Minorities* 4, July 1985.
6. *Western Mail*, 12 June 1919.
7. *Western Mail*, 13 June 1919.
8. *Western Mail*, 9 June 1919.
9. *Western Mail*, 16 June 1919.
10. On Sheikh Ahmad, see Martin Lings, *A Muslim Saint of the Twentieth Century*, London 1958.
11. A *zawiya*, literally a corner or nook, is used in Sufi Islam to denote a small mosque where a religious order has its centre. *Zawiyas* are found in North Africa, not in Yemen, but the Yemenis in exile have taken over the practice.
12. Collins, *op.cit.*, p. 180.
13. *Western Mail*, 6 May 1938.
14. *Al-Salam* (article in English as here), 25 May 1952.
15. Quoted in Collins, p. 225.
16. The text of this speech and the details on al-Hakimi's stay in Aden on his return are taken from an article by his son, Abd al-Rahman Abdullah al-Hakimi in *al-Hikma*, Aden, no. 44, 1 October 1975. His family claim al-Hakimi was poisoned by an agent of the Imam. Further details in Leigh Douglas, *The Free Yemeni Movement 1935–1962*, Beirut 1987.
17. *Al-Hikma*, pp. 68–9.
18. B. Dayha, 'South Asian Urban Immigration', unpublished Ph.D. thesis, University of London, 1967, Chapter VIII, 'Associations', pp. 315–24.
19. *Western Mail*, 8 October 1946 reported the arrival of the two princes in Cardiff. The title, 'Seif al-Islam', literally the 'sword of Islam', is that conventionally applied to the sons of a Yemeni imam.
20. *The Shields Daily Gazette and Shipping Telegraph*, 5 February 1919.
21. Extensive analysis in Dave Byrne, 'The 1930 "Arab Riot" in South Shields: A Race Riot That Never Was', *Race and Class* 3, 1977.

22. From correspondence in *The Shields Daily Gazette and Shipping Telegraph*, between 30 April and 13 May 1930.
23. *The Shields Daily Gazette and Shipping Telegraph*, 3 September 1930.
24. Sydney Collins, *Coloured Minorities in Britain*, London 1957.
25. *Migration To and From Merseyside*, Liverpool 1938, p. 10.
26. The first mosque in Hull was organized by Abdullah Hassan, a Shamiri who came to Hull around 1932 after living in Birmingham. He had a mosque in his house in Waverly St., from 1944 to 1959, and when this was demolished in redevelopment he moved it to a new house in Linnaeus St. Abdullah Hassan also ran a boarding house at Waverly St. See articles in *Hull and Yorkshire Times* 17 November 1945, 21 November 1953, 21 July 1956, 28 October 1966. In 1976 there were about fifty Yemenis left, most with British wives, congregating in the area around The Boulevard, off the fish docks. The Hull community had reached its peak during World War II and had then declined.

3   Yemenis in Industrial Cities

1. There is no definite number for the Yemenis in Britain. Dahya gives a figure of 12,000 for the early 1960s, a plausible guess.
2. This feature of Yemeni communities has also been observed in the USA. See Barbara Aswad, ed., *Arabic Speaking Communities in American Cities*, New York 1974, p. 62, where there is an account of the Yemenis in Dearborn, Detroit, and Jonathan Friedlander, ed., *Sojourners and Settlers*.
3. A few came after 1962, but they cannot have been more than 5–10 per cent of the total; they were mainly the sons of immigrants who were already in Britain.
4. See B. Dahya, 'Yemenis in Britain: An Arab Migrant Community', *Race*, 3, 1965. Dahya does not state that this study refers to Birmingham, but on the basis of his unpublished thesis it can safely assumed that it is this city to which the article refers.
5. E. J. B. Rose and others, *Colour and Citizenship, a Report on British Race Relations*, Oxford 1969, p. 174.
6. Madeleine Trebous, *Migration and Development, The Case of Algeria*, Paris 1970, p. 89.
7. Sheila Allen, Joanna Barrat, Stuart Bentley, *Work, Race and Immigration* unpublished manuscript, 1973, p. 53.
8. A gaffer is the word colloquially used for a foreman. Although there is a 'g' in spoken Yemeni Arabic (produced through hardening the

written 'j'), Yemeni workers usually pronounce the 'g' in gaffer with a *ghain*, possibly assimilating the word to the Arabic word *ghain-fa-ra*, meaning to guard or watch over.

9. See, for example, Rose, as note 5.

10. The housing conditions of Pakistani migrants in Birmingham have been graphically analysed in J. Rex and R. Moore, *Race, Community and Conflict: A Study of Sparkbrook*, Oxford 1967. While Sparkbrook itself was not an area of Yemeni concentration, many of the problems discussed by Moore and Rex applied to Yemenis in other parts of the city at that time.

11. On migrant women in Western Europe generally, see Godula Kosack, 'Migrant Women: The Move to Western Europe – A Step towards Emancipation?', *Race and Class*, Spring 1976. According to figures for 1966 the percentage of women working outside the home among British immigrant groups was: West Indians 75 per cent, Indians 41 per cent, Pakistanis 21 per cent. The comparable figure for British women was 45 per cent (*Racism: Who Profits?*, CIS Special Report, 1976, p. 22).

12. Until the early 1970s the main unit of currency in much of the hinterland of North and South Yemen was the silver coin, the Maria Theresa dollar, which was specially minted in Austria for the Middle East market. In the 1960s its average value was US\$ 0.80.

13. 'Yemenis Buy Way Into Britain', *Guardian*, 12 April 1976.

14. A report on South Yemen by a representative of the Swedish Save the Children Federation who visited the country in 1976 said: 'It is an interesting country which is very well organised in spite of its poverty. The country has real potentialities to receive and profit from assistance. We can be absolutely assured that each ounce of food gets into the right hands. Corruption does not exist.' *Dagens Nyheter*, 13 January 1976.

4. A Yemeni Workers' Organization

1. The best general discussion of the benefits and dislocations provoked by labour emigration of the contemporary kind is in Godula Kosack and Stephen Castles, *Immigrant Labour and Class Structure in Western Europe*, London 1974.

2. CEDETIM, *Les immigrés*, Paris, 1974.

3. For the reaction to 1962 among Algerian workers in France, see Madeline Trebous, *Migration and Development: The case of Algeria*, Paris 1970.

4. There is an account of the complex and changing relations between different nationalist groups prior to 1967 in my *Arabia without Sultans*, London 1974.
5. The BBC Arabic service is nearer, but it cannot be picked up in Britain itself, except with special receivers.
6. John de Witt, *The Indian Workers' Association in Britain*, Oxford 1969.

5   A Community in Transition

1. As part of this organization of the exile communities, periodic congresses of emigrants' representatives were held in Sana'a and Aden to mobilize support for the respective states, and their political and economic programmes.
2. Sheffield City Council, Employment and Economic Development Department and Race Equality Unit, *Yemeni Community Profile*, various reports, 1988–9.
3. On industrial illness see the main report, 'Work-related Ill Health in the Yemeni Community', in *Yemeni Community Profile*.
4. *Sheffield Star*, 30 September, 2 October, 3 October, 1989.
5. For a portrait of the Yemeni community in South Shields in 1989 see William Dalrymple, 'The Arabs of Tyneside', *The Independent Magazine*, 7 October 1989.
6. Michael Banton, *The Coloured Quarter*, London 1955, p. 13.
7. Banton, *op.cit.*, p. 96.
8. Peter Kalix, 'Khat: A Plant With Amphetamine Effects', *Journal of Substance Abuse Treatment 5*, 1988, pp. 163–9; Christos Pantelis, Charles Hindler and John Taylor, 'Use and Abuse of Khat (Catha Edulis); A Review of the Distribution, Pharmacology, Side Effects and Description of Psychosis Attributed to Khat Chewing', *Psychological Medicine* 19, 1989, pp. 657–68.
9. Panetelis *et al.* as note 8, p. 666.
10. *Observer*, 18 October 1987.
11. *The Lancet*, 20 February 1988, letter from Shelagh Weir and M. C. Thuriaux.
12. *The Economist*, 3 March 1990.
13. *Observer*, 20 December 1987.
14. Letter to *Guardian*, from M. A. Freeth, 21 January 1988.
15. For an analysis setting the issue in a Yemeni context, see Ianthe Maclagen, 'The High Cost of Getting a Bride in North Yemen', *Guardian*, 12 January 1988.

6 The 'Invisible' Arabs

1. W. Petersen, 'A General Typology of Migration', *American Sociological Review* 23, 1958, p. 263.
2. Muhammad Anwar, *The Myth of Return*, London 1979, p. 14.
3. Vaughan Robinson, *Transients, Settlers and Refugees*, Chapter Eleven.
4. Anwar, *op.cit.*, Chapter Five.
5. On incapsulation, see Anwar *op.cit.*, p. 15.
6. Jon Swanson, 'Sojourners and Settlers in Yemen and America', in J. Friedlander, ed., *Sojourners and Settlers*, p. 58.
7. Badr ud-din Dahya, 'South Asian Urban Immigration', unpublished PhD thesis, University of London, 1967, p. 332.
8. Anwar, p. 114.
9. On the diversities of 'Islam' and the contingent and variant interpretations of it with regard to social and political matters, see Fred Halliday and Hamza Alavi, eds, *State and Ideology in the Middle East and Pakistan*, London 1988.
10. Tomas Gerholm and Yngve Georg Lithman, eds, *The New Islamic Presence in Western Europe*.
11. The terms listed here are conventionally referred to by Yemenis (as well as others) as 'tribal'; in fact, they did not correspond to tribes, which tended to be smaller units, as much as to regions. Clearly the forms of affiliation and rivalry characteristic of these regional groups were similar to those of tribes, but it would be inaccurate to characterize them as tribes since, apart from other differences, they corresponded to no hierarchy or putative lineages.
12. Thus Little, *Negroes in Britain* (first published in 1947) and Collins, *Coloured Minorities in Britain* (1957). Even Dahya, whose thesis was on Yemenis alone, chose to entitle his work 'South Asian Immigration'. The term 'South Asia' has never been applied to the Arabian Peninsula, although the term 'South-West Asia' has, on occasion, been used.
13. Thus Banton in *The Coloured Quarter*, pp. 62–3.

Bibliography

1. The Yemeni Background

el-Attar, Said, *Le sous-développement économique et social du Yemen*, Algiers 1964.

Burrowes, Robert, *The Yemen Arab Republic: the Politics of Development, 1969–1986*, London 1987.

Gerholm, Tomas, *Market, Mosque and Mafraj*, Stockholm 1978.

Halliday, Fred, *Arabia without Sultans*, London 1974, Chapters 3–8.

—— *Revolution and Foreign Policy: The Case of South Yemen, 1967–1987*, Cambridge 1990.

Lackner, Helen, *PDR Yemen*, London 1985.

Peterson, John, *Yemen: The Search for a Modern State*, London 1982.

Pridham, Brian, ed., *Economy, Society and Culture in Contemporary Yemen*, Beckenham 1985.

Stookey, Robert, *South Yemen: A Marxist Republic in Arabia*, London 1982.

Weir, Shelagh, *Qat in Yemen: Consumption and Social Change*, London 1985.

Wenner, Manfred, *The Yemen Arab Republic: Development and Change in an Ancient Land*, Oxford 1991.

2. Yemeni Migration

Abraham, Nabeel, 'The Yemeni Immigrant Community of Detroit: Background, Emigration and Community Life', in Nabeel Abraham and Samir Abraham, eds, *Arabs in the New World: Studies on Arab–American Communities*, Detroit 1983.

Birks, Stace and Clive Sinclair, *Arab Manpower*, London 1980.

Bisharat, Mary, 'Yemeni Farmworkers in California', *MERIP Reports* 34, January 1975.

Dweik, Badr, *The Yemenites of Lackawanna New York: A Community Profile*, Council on International Studies, SUNY, Buffalo, Special Studies Series 130, 1980.

Friedlander, Jonathan, ed., *Sojourners and Settlers: The Yemeni Immigrant Experience*, Salt Lake City 1988.

Gilad, Lisa, *Ginger and Salt: Yemeni Jewish Women in an Israeli Town*, Boulder, Co. 1989.

Kostiner, Joseph, 'The Impact of the Hadrami Emigrants in the East Indies on Islamic Modernism and Social Change in the Hadramaut during the 20th Century', in R. Israeli and A. Johns eds., *Islam in Asia*, Jerusalem 1984.

Lackner, Helen, 'Labour Migration and its Socioeconomic Impact on the Sending Areas', unpublished M.Sc. thesis, Department of Social Science and Administration, London School of Economics, 1985.

MERIP Middle East Report, 'Sojourners and Settlers: Yemenis in America', no. 139, March–April 1986.

Myntti, Cynthia, 'Yemeni Workers Abroad: The Impact on Women', *MERIP Reports*, vol. 14, no. 5, June 1984, no. 124.

Swanson, Jon, *Emigration and Economic Development: The Case of the Yemen Arab Republic*, Boulder 1979.

3.   Migration and Race Relations in Western Europe

Amin, Kanshika, Fernandes, Maris, and Gordon, Paul, *Racism and Discrimination in Britain: A Select Bibliography 1984–87*, London 1988.

Allen, Sheila, Bornat, Joanne and Bentley, Stuart, 'Work, Race and Immigration', unpublished manuscript, 1974.

Anwar, Muhammad, *The Myth of Return: Pakistanis in Britain*, London 1979.

Bussne, L. and Drew, D., *Sheffield's Black Population: Employment – 1981 Population Census Statistics*, Sheffield 1985.

Castles, Stephen and Wallace, Tina, *Here for Good*, London 1984.

CEDETIM, *Les immigrés*, Paris 1971.

Dixon, Conrad, 'Lascars, the Forgotten Seamen', in Rosemary Omer and Gerard Panting, eds, *Working Men Who Got Wet*, St. John's, Newfoundland, 1980.

Gerholm, Tomas and Lithman, Yngve Georg, eds, *The New Islamic Presence in Western Europe*, London 1988.

Gordon, Paul and Klug, Francesca, *Racism and Discrimination in Britain: A Select Bibliography, 1970–1983*, London, (n.d.).

Gordon, Paul and Reilly, D., 'Guestworkers at Sea', *Race and Class*, Autumn 1986.

Halliday, Fred, 'The Struggle for the Migrant Soul', *Times Literary Supplement*, 6 June 1989.

Kepel, Gilles, *Les banlieues de l'Islam: Naissance d'une religion en France*, Paris 1987.

Kosack, Godula and Castles, Stephen, *Immigrant Labour and Class Struggle in Western Europe*, London 1974.

Krausz, Ernest, *Ethnic Minorities in Britain*, London 1972.

Madan, Raj, *Coloured Minorities in Britain, A Comprehensive Bibliography, 1970–1977*, London 1979.

Merseyside Area Profile Group, *Racial Discrimination and Disadvantage in Employment in Liverpool in 1986*.

Phizaclea, Anne and Solomos, John, *The Employment of Migrant Labour in Britain: A Select Bibliography*, 1984.

Rex, John and Moore, R., *Race, Community and Conflict: A Study of Sparkbrook*, Oxford 1967.

—— *Race and Ethnicity*, Milton Keynes 1986.

Robinson, Vaughan, *Transients, Settlers and Refugees: Asians in Britain*, Oxford 1986.

Rose, E. J. B., and others, *Colour and Citizenship: A Report on British Race Relations*, London 1964.

Stubbs, Michael, ed., *The Other Languages of England*, London 1985.

Trebous, Madeleine, *Migration and Development: The Case of Algeria*, Paris 1970.

Visram, Rozinna, *Ayas, Lascars, Princes*, London 1986, Chapter 3 'Sailors Who Filled the Gap: The Lascars'.

de Witt, John, *The Indian Workers' Association in Britain*, Oxford 1969.

4. Yemenis in Britain

Bailey, Martin, 'Death in the Steelworks', *Observer*, 21 January 1989.

Banton, Michael, *The Coloured Quarter*, London 1955.

Birmingham Evening Mail, 'Midland Money for Yemen Guns', 3 June 1964.

Byrne, Dave, 'The 1930 "Arab Riot" in South Shields: A Race Riot that Never Was', *Race and Class* 3, 1977.

Collins, Sydney, *Coloured Minorities in Britain*, London 1957.

—— 'The Muslim Family in Britain', *Social and Economic Studies* 4(4), 1955.

Dahya, Badr ud-Din, 'South Asian Urban Immigration, with Special Reference to Asian Muslim Immigrants in the English Midlands', University of London, PhD Thesis, no. 576, London 1967.
—— 'Yemenis in Britain: An Arab Migrant Community', *Race*, 3 January 1965.
Dalrymple, William, 'The Arabs of Tyneside', *The Independent Magazine*, 7 October 1989.
Evans, Neil, 'Regulating the Reserve Army: Arabs, Blacks, and the Local State in Cardiff, 1919–1945', *Immigrants and Minorities* 4(2), July 1985.
Guardian, 2 January 1989, 'Yemenis forge a stronghold in the city of steel by tempering tradition with youthful spirit'.
Hiro, Dilip, 'Three Faces of Tiger Bay', *New Society*, 21 September 1967.
Little, K. S., *Negroes in Britain*, 2nd edn, London 1972.
—— 'Loudoun Square: A Community Survey', Pts 1 and 2, *Sociological Review* xxxiv, nos 1 and 3, 1942.
Lloyd, D., 'Down the Bay', *Picture Post*, vol. 47 no. 2, 22 April 1950.
Macdonald, Eileen, *Brides for Sale? Human Trade in North Yemen*, Edinburgh 1988.
Serjeant, R. B., 'Yemeni Arabs in Britain', *The Geographical Magazine* 17(4), 1944.
Sha'if, Abdul-Qalil, 'The Yemeni Community' in Shiblak, Abbas, *The Arabs in Britain*, London 1991.
Sheffield City Council, Department of Employment and Economic Development, *Yemeni Community Profile*, 1988–9.

Index